LOVE, MARRIAGE

&

EVOLUTION

AMY EDELSTEIN

Love, Marriage & Evolution

Copyright 2013 by Amy Edelstein

ISBN 0615966292
ISBN 13 9780615966298

Published by Emergence Education Press

www.amyedelstein.com

Cover Art by Dorith Teichman

www.dorith-teichman.com

Cover Design by Free Agency

www.choosefreeagency.com

All rights reserved. Except as permitted under the U.S. Copyright act of 1976, no part of this publication may be reproduced, distributed, or transmitted in any form or by any means, or stored in a database or retrieval system, without the prior permission of the Publisher.

Library of Congress Control Number: 2013952065

This book is dedicated to all the courageous Spirit-seeking souls who want to change culture from the inside-out.

It is also dedicated to my husband for his enthusiastic support and encouragement, and for endlessly making me laugh.

TABLE OF CONTENTS

	Introduction	7
Chapter 1	Expectations	21
Chapter 2	Love	41
Chapter 3	Agreements	61
Chapter 4	Success	73
Chapter 5	Fulfillment	89
Chapter 6	Trust	101
Chapter 7	Home	121
Chapter 8	Balance	139
	What's Next?	153

INTRODUCTION

I embarked on this project because I feel strongly about the need for a sane and profound context for romantic relationships. Marriages should be happy, intimate, loving, fulfilling, significant, and meaningful examples of what's possible between people. I don't see any reason why they can't be. Marriage can be an inspiring and forward looking pillar of society rather than a throwback to a more restricted era and ethic. It can be beautifully based on future-oriented principles with a sacred foundation. If we keep this aspiration in sight, we can define a context and a way to be together that's deeply inspiring in a culture where there's so much insecurity, fear, and angst around what it means to be committed, together.

I have thirty years of experience in spiritual practice and a longstanding interest in cultural development. My initial quest started with mystical Judaism, philosophy, and ethics (mixed with some East-meets-West early pioneers) then in the 1980s I immersed myself in practice with some of the contemporary masters of Vedanta and Buddhism in Asia. I also spent over twenty-five years practicing evolutionary enlightenment with Andrew Cohen, and mentoring many people in their ongoing spiritual transformation. I am now an educator, working with many ages and backgrounds, in a variety of professional and academic environments, where I apply the principles of a spiritually informed evolutionary perspective to the values and ethics of contemporary life. I am committed to helping bring some of the seeming esoteric sensitivities and sensibilities into the mainstream, for after all, spiritual transformation has always been about the discovery and growth into our higher human potentials. And what could be better than that in any sector of society?

For many people in our increasingly urban postmodern culture, marriages or intimate committed relationships are where we go for spiritual congregation and support. We rely on our partners to be an anchor for us, a touchstone for meaning. We depend on them more than our friends, our professional groups, our yoga or meditation classes. Our marriages can provide grounding in that which is deeper, more sacred, more essential. They are a powerfully influential area of life. All the more reason we want to liberate this arena from unhelpful (and we'll find unnecessary) stress, tension, alienation, and static and transform our marriages into arenas of Spirit, heart, and depth. My goal is to support as many people as possible to experience this, and discover the vibrancy and uplift that results. When we live with more intentionality, trust our higher aspirations more fully, we are able to contribute to the world from a foundation created out of the inherent fullness and joy of Life, a life well lived.

My husband and I and I decided to get into a relationship in 2006, after knowing each other for over twenty years. We've been deep friends and companions on the path, and traversed much of the unfamiliar territory getting to know each other as friends, before we became romantic partners. We'd done years of spiritual practice side by side.

As you can see, we weren't exactly the childhood sweethearts or a later-life well considered match, but we share many similarities. We're friends, familiar like family. We're like-minded and self-assured. And we have space for each other. There's a beautiful Sanskrit phrase I always loved, *kalyana mitra*, which means spiritual friends. In close relationships, regardless of how much passion and romance there also is, I believe that spirit of *kalyana mitra* is the mortar holding strong a lasting foundation.

When I first started writing and creating coursework for *Love, Marriage & Evolution* I realized that we hadn't spend any time "working on" our relationship. As I reflected on that somewhat odd fact, I realized it calls into question many of our culture's fixed ideas about what creates closeness.

We spend a lot of time talking, debating, and sharing our insights on the numinous, exploring what enlightenment is, what we feel is most important in life, what it means to keep evolving, what new capacities exist in consciousness, and what the philosophers and spiritual masters we're currently delving into think about these same subjects. Like Talmudic or Tibetan debaters, he and I argue and passionately explore our beliefs about truth and revelation.

Now that I am working directly with couples, my husband and I do reflect quite a bit, turning over the ideas, values, meaning, future, changes, and intention of our marriage to understand what it all means and what the ebbs and flows are that keep the ever-renewing spring of consciousness fresh and bubbling forth. It's from this spring that I've developed the insights and guidelines you'll find in this book. I hope these insights help you discover a way of being together that is more easeful and delightful, more transformational and more catalytic than we've come to expect from all good marriage can be.

In This Book

Throughout, I use the term marriage somewhat loosely. I like the word because it implies dedication and commitment in relationship, though I am not particularly biasing the institution of marriage over couples who are together without being legally "married." I use the word to express and imply an intentionality in being together.

The perspective I'm sharing offers support regardless of whether we are in a long-term relationship, beginning a new one, single, or transitioning out of a long-term commitment. *Love, Marriage & Evolution* provides insight into ways to develop together, guidelines to help us create community, inspiration to enter into the right relationship by building shared agreements for mutual fulfillment, intimacy, trust, and transformation. It provides perspective so if you are in a new romance, you will be able to soar with the emotions while not losing your head in the thin atmosphere. If you are transitioning out of a long-term situation, you'll be better equipped to do so in a way that honors and respects the time you've spent together. We want to give as much value and significance as we can to what we've created and to slough off what has been not useful. By honoring our life experience and intimacies, we create the best possible circumstances to initiate a new phase of our lives.

The Questions We Have

I often get asked to help with sticky issues in people's relationships. The purpose of this book is to open up a context that will help you resolve those issues. This broader and deeper context supports a posture towards life that allows for more meaningful engagement with your partner and with the world around you. This orientation towards intimacy, shaped by an evolutionary and spiritually-oriented perspective, provides tools that build strength, resilience, and flexibility, necessary for any of us to navigate the challenges of life and of ongoing growth and transformation.

Love, Marriage & Evolution will give you a different sense of why our relationships are important and why we should care about what our marriages are expressing as the social constructs that they are. I'll address why looking at the values of our marriage with respect to the culture around us can actually help create space and peace in our personal experience with each other. And I'll talk about how to begin to look at ourselves and our intimate partnerships in this way.

Communication . . . most everyone wants to know how, what, and when to share their innermost questions with their partners. "How can I communicate in a more 'enlightened' way around difficult issues?" "Are there criteria to help me let go of what isn't helpful, useful, relevant, or important to bring up?" In our quest for the holy grail of intimacy, we all want and need to get to the higher clearing on the other side of the thorns so we can continue on the grand adventure of human evolution. Through learning the principles in *Love, Marriage & Evolution* you'll start to realize you have skills, tools, and a pathway through the foreboding briar patch of charged issues. Experience confidence in your own ability to navigate makes all the difference.

Another question many sensitive souls ask is, "How do I tap into my spiritual self so I can be different with my beloved?" "How can I shed my old skin, my old self?" Adopting a living spiritual perspective and making it our own is the foundation of the contemplations in this workbook. By recognizing a deeper aspect of the human experience, we can truly slough off old behaviors we've become habituated to. When we light up from within, inspired and captivated by something way beyond ourselves, we are lifted up on the wings of higher development. Carried above our old selves, we leave behind what has become outmoded or detrimental. As our attention becomes transfixed by more meaningful possibilities for our human life, we allow what is less significant to fall away, leaving us free to soar on the currents and contours of this new stratosphere of our own consciousness. Just as the earth's atmosphere gets thinner the further from the earth, as we embrace our higher capacities, we find ourselves lighter, needing less armor between us and the world. *Love, Marriage & Evolution* lays out an approach to reach a higher vantage point—one that gives us room to flower into fuller expressions of ourselves.

What To Expect

This book explores eight themes in relationships: Expectations, Love, Agreements, Success, Fulfillment, Trust, Home, and Balance. In each chapter, you'll learn about the theme and how it strengthens and brings more joy into your marriage and why it supports your own spiritual transformation. You'll also find specific questions for contemplation. Please do these. Working through these questions ourselves helps move us through our old beliefs. We progress, taking steps into a new way of seeing. Doing the contemplations together with our partners gives a center point to our work together, a way of practice whose focus and intention etches new grooves between us. The more you engage and work these questions, you'll start internalizing a deeper and broader view, and you'll practice the skills and perspective changes so they are familiar and at the ready when you need them most.

As we go through this process of inquiry, a context or container will start taking shape inside you, a place where you can hold the constantly changing dynamics and everyday particularities of your relationship. My goal is to free marriages of unnecessary stress and friction. As you begin to loosen the constrictions and delve more freely into this process of discovery, you'll experience a release of ease, affection, respect, security, trust, and aspiration, elements that bring—and hold—two people who love each other together.

My approach rests on an evolutionary understanding and a grounding in the mystical dimension of life. My aspiration is to uplift the context of marriage and to inspire and validate the spiritual stirring within. This will simultaneously demystify some of the common issues in relationship. By giving you tools and contemplations so you can make progress, I want to shift relationship work from one of sorting through issues and frictions to a shared inquiry that is wholly positive. Our relationship "work" can be a dynamic exploration of what supports our higher development. What is it between two people that creates a foundation of respect, honor, and ongoing creativity? What are the characteristics that lead to the bubbling up of joy and intimacy, trust and fullness, to more and more Love? We don't need to experience a lot of conflict to evolve, especially in our marriages. But if we do have periods of friction, we want to be confident that we can approach it as a natural unfolding of life, one that doesn't disturb the core of what we share with our partners. In offering you some of the best tools I've honed in my own decades of sustained and concentrated transformational work, I hope to ignite a recognition among us that our intimate relationships can be the very stuff of cultural evolution—and therefore, they hold the potential to change our culture significantly for the better.

Feel free to skip around the book, experiment with and adapt the contemplations, and make this your own process. Most importantly, have fun and enjoy! I am very encouraged by the immediate happiness, relief, release, respect, and love that people experience with *Love, Marriage & Evolution*. Our inspiration comes the direct experience of realizing that we really can become much better friends, partners, and lovers. We really can change our values, our attitudes, our consciousness. And when we change our consciousness, we change the currency of the culture between us, and that, is the stuff of change in our world.

In Spirit and for the future,

Amy Edelstein

Philadelphia, Pennsylvania

August 2013

CONTEMPLATIONS

What motivated you and inspired you to read this book?

_____

_____

_____

_____

What do you want to get out your engagement with it?

_____

_____

_____

_____

_____

_____

_____

_____

_____

Are you happy in your relationship but feel your relationship could be more oriented towards transformation, more meaningful, or more vibrant?

_____

_____

_____

_____

Are you in a relationship where you love each other but you feel that you're experiencing more conflict than is necessary? Articulate the connection and why you feel the prickles are more than necessary:

_____

_____

_____

_____

_____

Are you currently single and next time you enter into a relationship want to do it better than the last time?

_____

_____

_____

_____

Are you exiting a relationship and want to honor all that you have shared as you move on to a different chapter of your life?

_____

_____

_____

_____

Reflect on three things you'd like to be able to do differently in relationship:

_____

_____

1 EXPECTATIONS

We all have expectations in relationship. If we look, we find out, of course, that we have expectations in all areas of our lives. Mostly, our expectations are unexamined. We don't know exactly why we hold them, or whether or not the particular expectations we hold line up with what we most deeply believe and aspire to. In more cases than not, our desires, needs, aspirations, and goals are not created intentionally to mesh with our higher ideals. Unexamined expectations of marriage often go like this: We expect our partners to fulfill us. We expect to be relieved of an existential loneliness. We expect to become better people because now we're in love.

Rather than negotiate with these expectations, I'm proposing a different starting point. A different framework in which to think about your expectations of relationships. I'll lay out a way of ordering our values around the important issues to bring about a sustaining depth, alignment, and unity in your life.

What's Our Essential Purpose in Life?

What we expect from each other has to do with how we define the greater purpose of our lives and our marriages. Often times, we commit to each other without articulating what that union actually represents to us. Knowing what we stand for sets guidelines for how we want to be together. Those larger aspirations and principles create the framework for our lives. And they provide a beautiful goal to work towards *together*.

The first question to ask as we define expectations is, "What is the context within which I am looking for meaning and purpose? Is it primarily spiritual? Material? Philosophical? Values-based?" What is the goal that underpins all others that best encapsulates what I am striving for? What gets me going in the morning and happily keeps me up at night? If I could do anything, what would that be and more importantly, why?

When we're clear about the guiding values and aspirations of our life, and the context that guides us, we can prioritize what's important to us and shape our expectations in our marriage.

Sharing these goals and the passion and aspirations that shape them with our partners gives form to our love. When this becomes the currency between us, our deeper purpose, and the ideals that shape it, will be the rudder we depend on to navigate the currents of our life together with far more ease, fulfillment, and directionality.

Spirit & Life, Endlessly Unfolding

Establishing our relationships on our intimations of Spirit, discovering ways to come together in higher orders of unity, harmony, and complexity, and evolving the values that make up our culture are all qualities of the field or philosophy of "evolutionary spirituality." The guiding principles of this perspective grow out of the knowledge that we live in a continuously evolving universe; and this knowledge provides a context for our relationship with the numinous.

Sages, mystics, and philosophers over the last hundred and fifty years, from Emerson to Peirce, Kuuk to Aurobindo de Chardin to Swimme, Wilber to Cohen, and many others, have illuminated this perspective in far more depth and detail than I will do here. But what I will give you is a way to understand the broadest arc of these insights and how they can shape the expectations we create in our most intimate relationships.

Shared expectations that are based in a vast and deep context serve more than merely navigating the daily ups and downs. They set the fertile conditions for inner transformation, which then evolve the values of the culture we share.

Context Shapes Expectations—Being One with the Process of Evolution

To consciously set our own individual lives within the immense brushstroke of evolutionary unfolding is a powerful orientation for reaching toward our personal and spiritual ideals. And it's a powerful contextualization for marriage and relationship. We discover that we are non-separate from the incredible propulsion of creativity and life. We are not separate from the process of evolutionary unfolding. When we set our intimate life in that large a context, it repositions everything. Against that vast backdrop, how we navigate our finances, our personal idiosyncrasies, our likes and dislikes, and our moments of affection and intimacy shifts. The same instances, issues, and responses look very different. Sometimes entirely different.

Let's go through this more experientially. Picture the shiny flecks of the Milky Way scattered across the sky. Or imagine that you're telescoping in to the inside world of the nucleus of an atom, and you've gone in so far, you're swept up in the midst of all these tiny particles, quarks, pi-mesons, and gluons swirling around each other surrounded by incredible energy and light and little bits of matter. Visualize yourself as process, as part of the vast movement of the universe from the biggest scale of the formation of suns to the tiniest scale of nuclear particles, that's the stuff that we're made of. And that stuff is constantly reconfiguring at higher and higher levels of complexity and integration. That stuff has cohered and coalesced into human form and the human capacity of cognition and self-reflection. Then you will be able to recognize and acknowledge to yourself, "My emotional life, my self-identity, and my self-sense are intrinsically non-separate from that unfolding process, one that began so many eons ago and is equally non-separate from my partner asleep next to me!" You realize that many of the things that we tend to get tangled up in are just not that important. They're not that significant and they're not that profound.

I happen to relate to this form or body as me, and I happen to relate to my husband in his form, but when we telescope out and we see the reality and the nature of the evolutionary current, we recognize that an over-identification with us as separate selves is, from that vast perspective, almost nonsensical. That's what I mean when I say, focusing and framing a bigger perspective recontextualizes everything in our relationships.

Having a direct relationship with evolutionary unfolding is an important aspect of establishing a context that can inform and provide a sturdy framework. The minute we start putting our attention on process, we can see that it's the very stuff and substance that also brings us together with our partners. Part of our relationship is the creative and attractive quality of sexuality. In it you can feel the current and surge of the creative process. But what makes for successful relationship, I believe, is not some over-involved emphasis on perfecting the sexual encounter but rather understanding what the container or context of our relationship is. When we authentically relate to that container as life's vast and mysterious unfolding, there is infinite space to manage all the vicissitudes of life. This context significantly shapes and reshapes our expectations.

Does This Really Help When Times Are Tough?

A few years ago, I was in a very serious motor vehicle accident—an 18-wheel tractor-trailer and I met, nose-to-nose. Recently I overheard my husband describe his internal thought process right after he got the news. The EMT called with a perfunctory message, "Your wife has been in an accident. It's a Level 1 Trauma. She's being transported now to the Emergency Room." That was all the information they gave, other than the location of the trauma center. He got in the car to come see me with no idea what he was going to find.

My husband and I love each other very much. We're fast friends, partners in our life's work, and have always intended to have a long life exploring consciousness, spiritual transformation, and cultural evolution together. This event was oddly out of narrative and unexpectedly challenging.

On the way to the hospital, my husband found himself, because of the spiritual work we've been doing for so many years, instinctively running through the following thought process: He asked himself, "Do I still believe the evolutionary unfolding of the cosmos is a good thing? Is it positive at its essence? Is that my deepest understanding?"

In a split second, his more profound understanding of the nature of life came to the fore. He realized he really did know that the unfolding of creation with all its myriad events—its magnificent starbursts and little deaths—was in essence wholesome. He experienced the always-present awareness or infinite consciousness, its stillness and goodness moving through him. He found himself, in the midst of so much upheaval, on firm ground in a way he couldn't deny. In that instant, he said, he knew if the worst happened, "My life would suck—but the universe would still be good." And he knew whatever came, he would have the inner resources to respond. Whatever the future was going to be, he wouldn't be moved from his own realization of the inherent positivity of the universe's unfolding process.

CONTEMPLATIONS

Take a minute to let in the power of this kind of evolutionary awakening, the power of recognizing ourselves as process, as the impulse of evolutionary unfolding. Get in touch with that sense that there is so much more to unfold in the future that is way beyond our daily plans, our to-do lists, our accomplishments, our unfinished projects, our regrets. What has yet to unfold in front of us are new ways of seeing, perceiving, communing, intuiting, new ways of coming together, new understandings.

Now call to mind the last thing you got irritated about in your relationship. It could be a serious issue, or it could be a petty, mundane one. How does it look to you after having connected with that bigger context? Do you see how you might respond differently? Write down a few of your thoughts. This is a powerful reorientation, making it your own will take some time and focus.

_____

_____

_____

_____

_____

Only One Context for Your Life & Relationship

The way I see it is this: The context for your life is the context for your relationship. There aren't two separate contexts. There aren't two separate sets of rules. There aren't two separate goals or two separate sets of ideals. This can be as unsettling as it is meaningful. It sounds simple. It sounds straightforward. It sounds logical. It sounds easy to do. So why is it so paradoxically grounding and unnerving?

Because it takes our whole life and throws it into a structure as vast as the unfolding process of the universe. It is unifying. We're not used to experiencing such an all-inclusive unity. We're used to living our relationships in a much smaller context, where we manage all kinds of lesser expectations, and debate and negotiate over so many daily issues. We still will have those issues to negotiate. But when we've cast our mold in that which can't be contained, and we share that with our partners, there's infinite room and space to find all kinds of creative solutions and pathways together.

There really is no limit to the life challenges or the life successes that this perspective can help us with and carry us through. When we're giddy with joy, we want to maintain the right relationship to our relationship. When we're challenged by loss or fear, we want to maintain the right relationship to our partners. We want a steadiness and intimacy that is resilient and that easily flows and fluctuates as the circumstances in our lives change.

Discovering Depth

Our expectations come out of the context we frame our lives within. How vast that context is determines what we expect from our relationships. We looked at process, and at how our existence occurs in an immense unfolding of matter, energy, life, and consciousness. Mystical realization points us to the discovery of an endless depth of Self, of presence, of Being. Many people have had glimpses of infinitude, Spirit, of a sense of God or the timeless nature of the universe. These glimpses may have been

prompted by spiritual practice or may have come unbidden when we were young, racing breathlessly across a sun-soaked field. Even if we can't locate the catalyst in time, we can allow ourselves to assume that this knowing is present within.

When we allow ourselves to realize anew that our nature is not separate from the dimension of Self that we can't touch but that we know as surely as we know ourselves to be alive, we discover a very different orientation to others. We discover an essential liberation from lack, from the bondage that comes from insatiable desire and longing, from perceiving another as a servant for our needs. When I am rooted in a knowledge of wholeness and my spouse is too, our coming together is characterized by Love meeting Love, Self meeting Self, wholeness meeting wholeness. And our mutual expectation is to merge together as two inherently full beings—no clinging, no lack. No reason not to be close. No fear of abandonment.

When we are rooted in the recognition of Unity—what Vedanta calls Brahman or the "One without a second," what the Desert Fathers called "being in Christ," what Walt Whitman called "cosmic consciousness," and what mystical traditions refer to by a variety of names—Being, Emptiness, Fullness, the Unborn, the Deathless, the infinite—we realize there is no separation, no boundaries. There really is no other. There's no one separate from you and no one to be separate from. There's nothing missing from you that anyone else could possibly fill because, ultimately, at this fathomless depth of Self, no boundaries or limits or walls exist.

Non-separateness is something we can picture. Do you remember being a child, lying on your back and looking up at the night sky, wondering how it all works? You see the blackness and it has no end. But then you think it has to end somewhere. But if it ends, what comes after? Expanding the metaphor, that blackness of the night sky is somehow deeper than, untouched and unaffected by the stars or whatever objects seem to pass through its boundarilessness. That image of the night sky behind the stars is a perfect metaphor for our intimation of something beyond, an ever-present awareness, an unbroken dimension of Being or Self that underlies all of the world of form and time, all of the births of matter and life.

The power of this Self-recognition is profound. Putting our attention there creates a sense of respect, space, depth, awe, mystery, fullness, emptiness, and not knowing. It anchors us when we are intoxicated with the bliss and the chemical explosion that occurs when we get into a new relationship. It steadies us when we're letting go of relationships. We find ourselves at one with ourselves, non-separate from that infinite expanse, not lacking, not troubled no matter what may be occurring in our lives. This is a powerful context for relationship.

CONTEMPLATIONS

Sit in a comfortable position with your spine erect. Allow your attention to fall into yourself. Be easy, relaxed, and aware while softening your inner gaze. Allow the boundaries of yourself to become more porous, almost like a mesh or screen. With your inner eye become aware of a lack of separation between you and the air around you, the chair or cushion under you. Rest in this awareness for a few minutes.

Bring your attention back and pull to the forefront a recent memory or image of an experience of lack that you've had. Notice the two levels or dimensions of self—one self who is very aware of emotional need and one self who is transparent or porous with everything around and within. See the difference in how you can relate to your feelings of need. Write down what you are observing. Write down how this can change your expectations of what you want from your partner, which part of yourself you want them to support and affirm, and how you want to be there for them.

_____

_____

_____

_____

_____

Can We Expect Our Relationship

To Be Free of Neediness, Fear & Attachment?

How do we deal with our own neediness, our own grasping, our own longing and desire to get something for ourselves from another? Is there really an easy answer? How do we fundamentally rid ourselves of some kind of compulsive emotional clinging? Can we resolve fear and insecurity and keep our relationship clear and clean? Can we come to peace with the emotional states that knock us off balance, and compel us to do things we regret, to manipulate, suffocate, bully, or cajole? Is it possible to fulfill a shared expectation of a relationship free of this kind of strife?

I believe that yes, we can. We can live according to expectations of a relationship free from this kind of kilter. That's when we work with context. From my vantage point, the best way to deal with these issues is from their root. We do that by more deeply contemplating a source or context that is so vast and complete that these emotional reactions lose their sway over us.

When we ground ourselves in a deeper reality of the inherent fullness of Being, our emotional clamoring looks very different. In that reality, we know we can never satiate any need in another, because we are not separate from them to be able to "fill" them. And they are never separate from us, or from all that exists, nor are they lacking anything. If you delve deeply enough into your experience, this is what you will discover. And when you discover this ground, the "how" to respond to emotional issues will unfold as they arise.

Can We Expect to Be Happy All the Time?

When it comes to expectations or shared context, one question that often arises is how can we maintain a sweetness or humility with our partners given the pressures of life—tensions from work, financial instability, raising children, studying? When we're rooted in a big enough context and a deep enough sense of self, we won't lose perspective. It really is the only way around the conundrum of maintaining a center in what can be a very chaotic world. Remaining open and loving is directly connected with where we're rooted.

My husband and I are not always "happy," but we're not unhappy with each other. We can be going through a tremendous amount of tension related to objective circumstances and be frustrated by different things and talk about those frustrating things together, and express frustration as we're articulating the different issues—but we're not frustrated with each other.

If you're in deep partnership, you don't have to have a loving "feeling" all the time; life isn't always like that. Life is sometimes a pain. But you can be so deeply together and so much in partnership that the fact that life is frustrating or frightening or difficult at times doesn't have to create difficulty between you two.

The romantic relationship is one area of life where we can tangibly see how the principles of a spiritually awakened, evolutionary view work to bring our lives into a bigger embrace, and how that broader framework can make a profound difference in practical ways. When we share this vast context, and the expectations of development, love, and awareness, it puts our petty differences and annoyances into perspective.

It helps us work together with our loved ones for a common purpose rather than working on each other. It fills our consciousness with a sense of awe and humility, helping us to appreciate each other. We can be intimate and loving in our relationship, and in awe, together, of the ineffable and the wondrous.

In my experience working with people in this area of life, this perspective has had remarkable effects grounding spirituality in a hands-on life process. It scoops up the stuff of our lives and elevates it, bringing the magnificent into our rational awareness.

Expectations of Sensitivity & Compassion

Some people have asked me, "Doesn't expanding our perspective and sense of consciousness that widely make us less sensitive, even callous, to our partners?" As we look into our experience contemplating oneness, we become engulfed with a compassion and awareness around our humanity. We recognize that we are, in many respects, fragile creatures. We become attuned to our own humanity. And this hollows out a deeper, inner reservoir for care.

What does it mean that we are fragile, complex creatures? How does that sensitivity relate to the process perspective we've been speaking about? Looked at in an evolutionary context, human beings are more complex, more developed than earlier life forms, and that complexity goes hand-in-hand with fragility. Like the workings of a finely tuned watch, complex organisms are highly sensitive, with interconnected systems that can be easily thrown off. There are far sturdier and simpler creatures than us. Take sea turtles, for example, which have been around for about 230 million years and are one of the oldest reptiles on Earth. They appear far earlier than humans on the evolutionary family tree and the functioning of their structure and biological systems is hardier than ours. Humans have a far more intricate cognitive system. In that sophistication lies vulnerability. That means we have to take care. We have to be sensitive to each other's humanity and avoid trampling on each other's trust.

Trust is fragile. Communion is fragile. Realization is fragile. As we grow to appreciate the delicacy of the evolutionary trajectory our capacity for empathy increases. It's a natural response as we awaken to and appreciate the beauty of creation.

Recognizing our place on Earth as part of the vast process of evolution instills in us a sense of awe and respect. When we shape our expectations out of that recognition, it infuses our relationship with care, compassion, and Love. We develop a sensitivity. We instinctively want to honor appropriate boundaries, and respect and value each other.

Expectations of a Greater Purpose—It's Not Just for Us

Our camaraderie, intimacy, support, and affection can be a powerfully uplifting example in culture. The way we are together, the currency or consciousness of our relationship, can be a steadying force for the society around us.

Caring about the example we set in culture, becoming a light of awakened evolutionary sensitivities, changes the expectations we have of each other and of our partnerships. Our marriages become important—how we work together on these deeper mystical goals, the joy we experience in each other's company, and the increasing and ever-expanding presence of greater and greater care and Love. From that place, we work together, not on each other, and all kinds of possibilities open up between us. Our well-being becomes the culture's well-being. And that's a steadying context to set our relationship in.

Sometimes people ask me what a truly future-oriented and spiritual relationship looks like. At this stage of cultural development, we are each pioneers. The stuff of our family history and cultural habits, and the idiosyncrasies of our personal nature, will dictate certain preferences. All of our relationships will each look a little different because of these factors. That's the thrill and the beauty of being intrepid pioneers of development at this moment in human history. Until we are five hundred, a thousand, ten thousand couples who truly share a process-oriented perspective with profound spiritual sensitivities, we're all explorers of the possible, creating, through our own relationships, examples of what we, as partners, can be. And as those new habits emerge in our intimate relationships with our partners, they become the stuff of cultural change.

2 LOVE

When I was planning this chapter, I had Tina Turner's song "What's Love Got To Do With It?" playing in my head. In personal transformation circles that frame development in an evolutionary context, an overemphasis can be put on emergence. In those cases, love of one another, of the Divine, and of our larger fellowship can often be unceremoniously disregarded. While I am not going to elevate the drama of interpersonal romance nor tout the virtues of impersonal love that turn a blind eye to our affections for each other, what I will do is show you a way to relate to your loved one in the context that we discussed in the last chapter. A bigger framework keeps things in perspective while fostering intimacy, just as a careful gardener tends a lush flowerbed.

In the last chapter, we explored the fact that the context for our life is the context for our relationship—there's only one context. As we engage with the breadth and depth of a process oriented spiritual context, our expectations in our personal relationships change. With an evolutionary worldview we simply take in more than we customarily do, telescoping way out in order to include the entire unfolding of the universe from the simplest forms of matter and energy to complex cognitive functioning. That's a huge swath of time and development. When most of us go through a refocusing of the context we set ourselves in, we immediately experience space, a wholesome reordering of all the different aspects of our lives. It brings a wonder and awe into our worlds and a smoothing out of static that can be generated when we become overly familiar with our partners.

A spiritual or awakened experience of life similarly reframes our worldview. A powerful realization of Oneness, fullness, or emptiness eliminates our identification of ourselves as separate from others. We often experience a flooding of Love through our being, wiping away all sense of lack, alienation, or longing. It changes how we approach more surface layer feelings of need and attachment in relationship. It instills a confidence and surety in our experience of the goodness of life and of the power and presence of Love.

When you were engaging with the contemplations from the last chapter, did you start to feel some space, some freedom? Some queasiness? Did you find yourself questioning, "If I let go of my needs, then what does that really mean about my self-sense? What does that mean about my expectations in perspective while fostering intimacy, just as a careful gardener tends a lush flowerbed.

In the last chapter, we explored the fact that the context for our life is the context for our relationship—there's only one context. As we engage with the breadth and depth of a process oriented spiritual context, our expectations in our personal relationships change. With an evolutionary worldview we simply take in more than we customarily do, telescoping way out in order to include the entire unfolding of the universe from the simplest forms of matter and energy to complex cognitive functioning. That's a huge swath of time and development. When most of us go through a refocusing of the context we set ourselves in, we immediately experience space, a wholesome reordering of all the different aspects of our lives. It brings a wonder and awe into our worlds and a smoothing out of static that can be generated when we become overly familiar with our partners.

A spiritual or awakened experience of life similarly reframes our worldview. A powerful realization of Oneness, fullness, or emptiness eliminates our identification of ourselves as separate from others. We often experience a flooding of Love through our being, wiping away all sense of lack, alienation, or longing. It changes how we approach more surface layer feelings of need and attachment in relationship. It instills a confidence and surety in our experience of the goodness of life and of the power and presence of Love.

When you were engaging with the contemplations from the last chapter, did you start to feel some space, some freedom? Some queasiness? Did you find yourself questioning, "If I let go of my needs, then what does that really mean about my self-sense? What does that mean about my expectations in my marriage?" Questions like those inevitably get triggered when we start to walk a transformational path like this one. A spiritual and evolutionary worldview unseats our familiar notions of self and reprioritizes many of our values. Explore these questions with your partner. Open up the assumptions you hold. See what you discover in this interesting new inner landscape.

Now let's reflect on what love is.

CONTEMPLATIONS

Do you tell your partner you love them very frequently?

___

Do you believe you're too attached to your partner if you miss them when you're apart?

___

Do you feel you don't care enough about your partner if you don't miss them when they're away?

___

Do you believe that however you feel in those situations doesn't necessarily indicate one thing or another about the depth of your bond?

___

Love's All Right with Me

As I've laid out, the path of transformation, and the realizations we pursue alter our worldview, our sense of self, our values and priorities, and our relationships with each other. When it comes to defining and understanding love, this transformation of self sense has far-reaching implications. Once we intimate a non-separateness with all that is, discovering oneness as consciousness and oneness as process, we realize an unexpected and undeniable fullness at a deep level of ourselves. We sense a unity with all that is, which includes with our partner asleep next to us. For some, this can create confusion. "I still love my partner, does this mean I haven't gone deeply enough to shift my values according to this realization of "no other at all"?" "I enjoy being with my partner, I don't want to dissolve that into the great sea of Love for all that is."

These are good questions and profound ones. My view holds our love for each other in our relationships in high regard. I see no need to do away with love between us, as a feeling, an attitude of endearment, or as a standard for the quality of our interactions with each other. What I do want to do is separate out this type of mature love, affection, friendship, and intimacy with our partners from many other more superficial uses of the same term. And especially from an understanding of love that reinforces ideas of attachment, fear, inadequacy, or objectification.

Love is a multi-purpose word in our culture. It's surprising that we never developed twenty different words like Inuit have for snow or Japanese have for rice. But for now, we'll have to work with the single appellation. When we commonly think about love between two people, it represents the desire to be connected, to interact and care, and to experience all the good things that come from that type of affection. And that same term can reference everything from fairy-tale liaisons to addictive soap-opera dramas, from commoditized sexuality to the vacuousness of a pop jingle. Just think about the last times you heard the word used—I love chocolate, I love NY, I love my car. We don't need to be afraid of using the word "love." It's not a bad word or a mere "personal" word or a word that only denotes some of our less enlightened postmodern characteristics—dependency, narcissism, or superficiality. The challenge of this contemplation we're undertaking here is to restore dignity and wholesomeness to our expectations of love, while adding a depth dimension. The added challenge is embracing the reality that opening up to greater and greater affection of another without falling into either an over-personalization or an objectification of our partner requires more self knowledge and inner honesty than it may at first seem.

Updating Love

They say love is as old as the hills. While it may be old, our understanding of love also regularly needs to be updated as we, and our capacities of consciousness evolve. To meet the shifting mores of our times and to reflect our more complex understanding of what it means to come together, we inevitably find ourselves in the midst of defining new norms, habits, and expressions of intimacy. As we embrace a spiritually awakened evolutionary worldview, we find ourselves writing a new edition of the book of love.

Our ideas of love are set by the society around us more than we may realize. While there are so many interpersonal elements and triggers, it's helpful to realize we can't think about love outside of the way the culture around us thinks about it. Like it or not, we bounce off of the ideas and iconic characterizations. If we adhere unconsciously to what we absorb, we're going to express love in a prescribed way, defined by traditions, habits, and preferences that have developed over the most recent fads, or over decades, centuries, millennia. Any expression outside of those norms will be seen as an inadequate or even aberrant expression of love. In the face of that pressure on us to conform, how independently are we engaging with our affection for our partners, and with the greater purpose of our lives?

All You Need Is Love?

As we look at how we want to update our understanding and expression of love, it's helpful to see the values that have just come before us. We're coming out of the "peace, love, and happiness" movement of the 1960s, which brought about a sex-positive attitude, compassion for others around the world, and for our planet and biosphere. In this movement, you find free-love revolutionaries, who embraced a spiritual context for their values and whose experience of cosmic Love gave them the courage to not just "love the one they were with" but also to transform our world. They inspired peace corps to feed the hungry, concerts to uplift the poor, medical missions to alleviate blindness, and other acts of love that moved mountains. The loosening of customs around coupling brought a more public tenderness into relationships, an empathy and respect for emotional sensitivity of both men and women. But the free love of the sixties and its association with spiritual awakening didn't create a utopian atmosphere and transform the world the way many hoped it would. More often than not, the free love ethos of that time got played out as a more culturally acceptable form of sexism. It held out a promise without a reliable enough means to deliver. We need an upgrade now, a more sophisticated understanding of the relationship between spiritual Love and interpersonal Love, between affection and attraction, coupling and caring, compassion and human evolution.

Love & Understanding

When it comes to love between people in a context of spiritual realization, there's no single recipe for how to be. Love is based more on alignment with our deepest understanding and greatest care, than it is on how we happen to feel at any particular moment. That's a subtle but powerful reorientation—and can do away with over-imbuing any particular moment in a marriage with undue significance or with a static expectation that we will never be able to create.

Becoming increasingly conscious of our experience, of the changing emotions and factors that generate love in any relationship, develops a multicolored palette of expression for our commitment and affection. Our priorities in life will ebb and flow. There's not going to be one fixed code that enables us to know in advance how to express a maturing of interpersonal love or a dawning revelation of more profound spiritual Love. We can track our development by how increasingly aware we become of the way our experience moves in us, what insights are emerging, and how those new discoveries are guiding our behavior and attitudes.

A Different Focus

There are different kinds of love in a marriage—love that we seem to instinctively feel for each other, a magnetism or chemistry, and love that's earned over time, through shared experience, and through the demonstration of our more noble natures to each other in times of trouble. Cultivate and nurture both kinds of love, respecting and honoring the bond that brought us together, respecting and honoring each other for the personal commitment, values, and higher purpose that's upheld.

There are also certain qualities and attributes of love that bring us together and actions or ways of being that strengthen and enrich the love between us. They include our value for and adherence to the path of development, our trustworthiness and commitment, our support and spaciousness, and our passion for the sacred in life.

The more we engage with inner transformation, the more we grow to appreciate how much courage we need to make progress on such a path. Changing culture from the inside out requires exceptional commitment. Recognizing this commitment in another generates love. When we see our partners engaging with the challenge of self-knowledge and the intention to affect positive change in the world around us, love becomes clothed in respect and honor for our partner's fortitude and willingness to struggle for inner independence.

How does this ideal look in the world of breakfast and bills? It looks like patience and forbearance. There may be aspects of our partner's personality or psychological structures that they will struggle with at some point in their development. And sometimes we will struggle to change for a period of time, maybe even years. This can create some strain at times. When we are committed to higher ideals, what we value in our partner is their intention, courage, and effort, and we will have patience through more difficult moments, extending support to see how their path unfolds over time.

Love of Spirit, Love of Each Other

When we embrace a spiritual path with the fullness of ourselves, our intention and spiritual curiosity can take us beyond anywhere we've known. Through effort or through grace, we can step off the cliff of the known and tumble headlong into a free fall of revelation. The love of God dissolves all separation, all difference, all other. Mystics seek to drown in Love and never return. "Inside love there is more joy than we know of," poet Kabir writes. Falling into that bottomless well of divine intoxication can overtake us.

When we awaken to the spiritual context of our lives and see a vaster way of relating to all existence, sometimes people feel they can't even use the word "love." They can't even relate to it anymore because it seems so partial, so much less than the magnitude and beauty and glory that we are awakening to. Expressing special intimacy or love of another can feel like a denial of this greater reality that is nearer than near, more present than our very breath or heart. It can feel like telling anyone in particular "I love you" would be in some way a denial of the larger context that we're newly in touch with.

This revelation is profound and beautiful. Still, it can be disconcerting to those we do indeed love. My pragmatic response to the intoxication experience of universal Love that comes from Spirit, is to drink of it responsibly, have care for those close to you. Know that movements of Love in us, including Divine Love, change in form, expression, intensity, and feeling. We can both allow ourselves to let go to the awakening of a spiritual love and take care of those around us.

The Stuff of Connection

Occasionally, when I start speaking about big perspectives, people express concern that this may trigger alienation in their relationship. "Can you leave your partner so much space that you lose connection with them?" When the space we give our partners is inspired by an evolutionary perspective, it is motivated by the desire to support each other's pace of development and to maintain an environment of respect in the home.

We lose connection with our partners if our fundamental values start to differ so vastly that we can no longer come together in a shared purpose. We lose connection when we stop respecting each other's depths and start relating to our partners more superficially. We lose connection when we become overly familiar with each other and lose the recognition and love of the sacred in the other. We lose connection when we forget the value we hold for each other's more noble aspirations. In these ways we can fall into a sense of distance that is unwholesome and not supportive of our partner's transformation, or our own.

What is supportive is the cultivation of respect and gratitude for one another. Gratitude and love really do go together. We love our spouses in part because we appreciate the companionship, the fun, the affection, the humor, the company, the support, and the food for thought that we receive from them.

These days both my husband and I are involved in so many creative projects that we often find ourselves light-heartedly competing for each other's attention, wanting to share our excitement over what we are discovering. We'll bounce back and forth from his arena to mine and share our thrill about what we're doing. We appreciate our connection and the opportunity to explore our interests and insights with each other. That's a powerful type of common purpose and it brings with it a wellspring of affection.

Of course all relationships ebb and flow in regards to bursts of creativity and verve. There will be times when the connection is more intense and others when it is quieter, more in the background. Setting your relationship in a big enough context allows for those changes, then love and commitment are not dependent on a uniquely exciting or dynamic time, but instead on recognition of a shared life mission that transcends the particulars.

A Sense of Well-Being

Love and commitment are intimately related. We're committed first and foremost to go as far as we can in our own development. By that I mean we're committed to becoming an embodiment of our deepest understanding and highest ideals. That commitment is solitary—between us and ourselves—and independent of whatever our partner does or doesn't do. That commitment also enables us to be truly committed in the relationship that we choose to be in.

Commitment in relationship is important. And I believe that in our contemporary culture it is neither sufficiently expected nor valued. I find it hard to separate love from commitment because whenever we get involved with each other, particularly intimately and sexually, there's a bond—a karmic connection, if you will—that's created between two people. When we develop bonds like that, we are more sensitive to those connections. It's how our emotional and biological structures work. Like it or not, how well—or unwell—our relationships are going, easily affects our capacity to focus on higher and more subtle areas of development and insight. Open channels and unobstructed communion provide us with a safety net that allows us to let go. A sense of well-being and ease enable us to create, explore, and experiment. If we yearn for ground from which to grow spiritually, the ability to trust and let go with the people we are closest to is all but essential. Strong mutual commitment and purpose provides that foundation. A synonym for this foundation and care for each other's higher development is love.

CONTEMPLATIONS

What do you feel the role of love is in a relationship? Spend ten minutes writing down your beliefs and ideals. Allow yourself to articulate different things that come to mind. Resist limiting your expression. List some creative ideas and images to provide a basis for continued reflection.

_____

_____

_____

_____

_____

_____

_____

_____

_____

_____

_____

During this week, pay attention to your experience. Make some notes about the aspects of love we discussed in this chapter including commitment, trust, and respect.

_____

_____

_____

_____

_____

_____

_____

_____

_____

_____

_____

_____

_____

_____

_____

Consider your ideal of balance and equality with your partner. Now consider your gauge of love. Do these two value sets work against each other? If so, makes some notes about how you could think about them differently.

_____

_____

_____

_____

_____

_____

_____

_____

_____

_____

_____

_____

_____

_____

3 AGREEMENTS

In this chapter, we're going to talk about the agreements we share with our partners. Defining our shared agreements in a way that leaves plenty of room for growth while establishing important values and boundaries will eliminate much of the unnecessary, petty friction that so often arises in relationships.

The qualities we've already covered will form the backbone of this next inquiry. In chapter I, we discussed the idea that the context for your life is the same context for relationship. Fundamentally, our life priorities and values, particularly if we're committed to spiritual development and to the transformation of culture, hold true for relationship too. The more conscious we are about that, the simpler the issues are going to be in our marriages.

We also explored how our relationships are to be lived more for the evolution of culture than for our own happiness. The goal of relationship, when we're committed to this kind of transformation, can't be just for ourselves (even though when we are committed in this way we will be much happier!). Rather, we want to provide an example of a union, partnership, and friendship that expresses deeper values. We want our example to be attractive, vibrant, vital, and constantly evolving so we can demonstrate to the existing culture that the principles of evolutionary unfolding and spiritual freedom can transform our lives and our relationships. Hopefully, we will, with our own lives, inspire others to pursue higher values. This is how we can change culture from the inside out.

In chapter 2, we explored love, and how the context in which we see ourselves—the unfolding of the evolutionary process, its principles of emergence and coherence, and our recognition of the always liberated Self—keeps our relationships from being too weighted in our history together, individual emotions, and interpersonal dynamics. When we understand that, we can freely express affection, commitment, trust, and concern for our spouses without descending into a dramatic, emotionally draining, hypersensitive expression of what often is mistaken for intimacy or love.

All you have to do is go to the grocery store to see couples who are obviously close with each other arguing and bickering about the most mundane and unnecessary things. We want to avoid that kind of friction. It's not helpful, not supportive, and it doesn't allow consciousness to soar.

We want to create conditions that allow us—as individuals and as a couple—to explore the edge of our spiritual understanding and of life's deeper questions. In this way, we can become "cultural attractors," for our friends, co-workers, even those who don't know us well. Our marriage will be an example to others of something that is nonexclusive but affectionate, intimate, dynamic, creative, stable, and ever evolving. Our agreements are what help us to create the environment for that kind of relationship to thrive.

While everyone will have to find their own way, and explore and discuss these and other agreements together, there are four basic ones that can be helpful to start with.

Shared Agreement: Respect the Foundation

We come together, we make a commitment, we become sexually involved with each other, and we commit to our partnership. We don't want to destabilize or question that foundation. We don't want to renegotiate that. Continually questioning that foundation creates a tremendous amount of insecurity and static in the background, preventing us from letting go into deeper levels of trust and exploration.

By respecting and honoring our mutual commitment, and by respecting and honoring our spouses for who they are independent of their relationship with us, we also express our respect for the larger context in which we love each other.

Shared Agreement: Give Each Other Space

We depend on our partners for so many things and we share so much together. Some people feel that the romantic context is our arena for personal work—that because we're so involved with each other, our partners are the best people to use as our mirrors and work out our personal knots. Not necessarily. This is subtle territory. Just because we live with our partners doesn't mean that they are our on-call therapist available 24/7, regardless of what's happening for them. We each have needs, rhythms, and flows. We're also each sensitive to how we feel with and are perceived by the other. Of course certain reactions get triggered. Caring about each other means we treat each other with respect and sensitivity. This agreement can have profound results in relationships.

It's essential that we truly recognize that our partners have their own lives, their own interests, their own involvements, their own concerns, their own pressures, and their own obligations. Therefore, we can't impose ourselves on them just because we're a "couple." This posture of respect allows our partner the freedom to be and to breathe, and for them to be there for us when we truly need their support. The more we respect each other's time, attention, and emotional space, the less chance there will be for miscommunication and the more opportunities to support each other.

It is so important to become sensitive to each other in this way. But this takes putting our attention on what's most important at the time, and letting go, renouncing our own neediness while bearing our own emotional insecurities and challenges. In short, it means being responsible for ourselves as the mature adults that we are.

Shared Agreement: Create Community

For many of us our closest spiritual "community" is with our partners, but it's unrealistic to rely on one relationship to support us in every aspect of our lives. Many of us have a healthy ambition when it comes to our inner development. We want to progress, we want to create, we want to evolve, we want to be examples. Learning how to do this with balance and grace, subtlety and flexibility in our closest relationships takes time and attention. It's a mission and goal that we can work on together, and learning how to do this (rather than working out our issues on each other) builds trust, love, appreciation, and gratitude.

If we're on a spiritual path and find ourselves challenged by something, for instance, personal idiosyncrasies that we need to change, we cannot simply dump this on our partner. There are times we need help to free ourselves of our blind spots. We'll need input from someone with vision and a vantage point higher than our own. Cultivating relationships with others who can provide that for us, developing a congregation, a sangha, a spiritual community that can offer that degree of clear vision will support us to go much farther and will make our own process of transformation and change one that is inspiring to our spouses. Working out this process with your partner alone puts enormous pressure on that relationship, which is simultaneously your sexual relationship, and often your financial relationship, and a source of love, affection, camaraderie, daily support, and companionship. That's a lot to impose on and expect from a single friendship.

We want to extend our network so that we have other committed relationships with peers who share a spiritual path. We can work with other friends in a deep way and then share these insights in our relationship, enriching it with unexpected growth. If you don't live in a spiritual community or have close spiritual friends with whom you feel sufficiently connected, then you're going to have to tread lightly with this one. You're going to have to think about ways to bring in respect and establish boundaries that protect your mutual development. Simultaneously, you might want to start looking for ways to extend your network while your partner does the same thing. Doing so will allow your marriage to become unexpectedly warm and fulfilling.

Shared Agreement: Trust Each Other's Intention

When you trust your partner's intention, you trust they are committed to spiritual transformation and you don't need to become their dharma police to make sure they stay focused on their own development. When you trust their intention to evolve, you don't have to force the issue. If you're expanding your network and working with others who are deeply committed to transformation you'll be able to enjoy a lightness of being, an ease, a security, and a peacefulness in your relationship founded on mutual trust in each other's ability to follow through on your own spiritual commitments.

Shared Agreement: Freely Extend Ourselves

There are a lot of ways to understand reciprocity. People sometimes relate to it as "quid pro quo"—a scale that weighs and dictates how much we'll trust. "I'll trust as far as you'll trust me. Prove to me that you're trustworthy." It seems simplistic but in contemporary culture, the dynamics of relationship generally turn on this kind of bargaining, a dynamic that can quickly devolve the relationship into something small and confined. In such a measured exchange, we'll only let go as much as we've seen the other let go. If the other's levels of letting go, trusting, and loving do not match our expectations then we reserve the right to withdraw—hardly a trusting or affectionate dynamic. A quid pro quo approach to relationship never comes from a liberated part of the Self that is always already full. When we have clear boundaries and we deeply respect each other, we can love without fear of being taken for granted or burning out.

Ongoing Agreements

It's an art to develop wholesome structure in the more freeform arenas of our lives. Remember the greater "why"—where we're heading in our relationship, what our goals in life are. Doing so will create a more wholesome environment between yourself and your partner. In such considerations, we want to keep our fundamental commitment to each in the forefront.

We may disagree on certain issues in life, sometimes even important ones. We may see things differently and have strong disagreements and have to wrestle them out together, but throughout the entire process we can fundamentally honor and respect the best qualities of each other, our commitment to each other, and the reasons why we got together in the first place.

We actually have to go against the tide of popular culture in order to create a relationship that's based on consistent and enduring trust.

CONTEMPLATIONS

The Shared Agreements we discussed in this chapter are intertwined and also work together as one:

1. Respect the foundation of your relationship. You got together for a reason, so you can honor your love and commitment, and each other's qualities.

2. Give each other space. Don't use each other to work out your ego issues. Our partners are our companions on the same path, not our on-call therapists.

3. Create Community. Work together and independently to expand your circle of friends and to create a supportive structure around you in which you both can flourish.

4. Trust each other's intentions in regards to spiritual transformation. Allow each other the space to develop. When it comes to inner transformation, some things take time.

5. Extend yourself. Focus on respect and care for each other and for the purpose-filled life you aspire to live.

Make conscious what your shared agreements are with your spouse. List the three you feel best define the parameters of your relationship:

_____

_____

_____

_____

_____

_____

_____

Are these agreements with your partner or are they expectations you hold for yourself?

_____

_____

_____

_____

Can you see a way to expand your circle of intimate/spiritual friends in a way that might take an unnecessary burden off your marriage/intimate partnership? Write down how you might cultivate a broader support circle:

_____

_____

_____

What would you like your relationship to express in 3 years? 10 years? 20 years? Make some notes of each milestone. Spend some time contemplating the deeper values you are committed to.

_____

_____

_____

_____

_____

_____

_____

_____

_____

_____

4 SUCCESS

How can we know that our relationship is going in the direction of a deeper realization and assimilation of spiritually awakened, future-oriented principles? What constitutes success? How can we know since the developmental path we've been discussing is far from codified?

An open interest emerges as we put our attention on these topics and question our assumptions. What I'm pointing to is not just care about my partner, my marriage and where I want to go, but what are we demonstrating in our relationships? How does our consciousness, our care about what we are expressing impact not just our partners, but also the other people we care about, those we touch in our lives? As we look at the qualities of success, these are some of the questions to consider.

Take note of how quickly you may have already begun to perceive a context—one that is fascinating, stabilizing, and developmental—for your relationship and your life. Can you see how working with this perspective will bear fruit in an arena that is so often fraught with fear, insecurity, uncertainty, and self-doubt? We do not need to live that way! Habits of our culture emphasize objectification, mistrust, over familiarity, and disregard in the landscape of intimate relationships. When we put our attention on a very different set of values, together we can create a much more sacred and future-oriented environment in which to live and develop. In this way, we can see how transformation in the dynamics of intimate relationships becomes a portal for cultural evolution. Now we will talk about what success looks like. What are the signs of success? How can we tell? As more and more of us align our marriages with these evolutionary insights, new understandings and expressions will emerge. Let's hold what follows loosely and adapt it as we work this new value set in the years and decades ahead.

Signs: Inclusivity

When it comes to relationships, the question arises, can we fall in love, be intimate with our spouses, and without creating an emotional barrier with a broader, more inclusive, collective communion?

A sign of success for a marriage in this context is inclusivity. As close as we are with our partners, our closeness would not exclude others. You often see exclusivity right when people fall in love. Think about adolescent lovers. They're happy. Very happy! So happy, they feel like the only ones who exist in the universe. When they're with others, they quiver with anticipation for that moment when they can finally be alone again and in each other's arms. The two become a unit, and everyone else becomes furniture in the room. The feeling of falling in love is delightful. There's a chemical reaction that explodes. It's beautiful to let go and feel that happiness. But the cascade of chemistry that ignites in our brains, bodies, and nervous systems doesn't have to define how we relate to the world around us. We can let go in love without narrowing down the quality of consciousness and the field we create together. We can be inclusive even as our affection opens up for our new lover.

Inclusivity also doesn't mean we invite the world into the intimacy we have with our partners. The sixties made it okay to "let it all hang out." But when you care about the subtler aspects of collective consciousness and development, respecting the boundaries between public and private, personal and collective space is vital. Decorum is a beautiful value, and a sign of emotional and spiritual maturity. Decorum, time alone with our loved ones, and warmth and inclusivity can all co-exist.

When we're very close with our spouses, when we are one in higher purpose and calling, other people will find themselves drawn. It can actually bring people together and spread faith, optimism, and positivity. With so much instability in our culture it's attractive when we see couples sharing a warmth that's not inhibited or contrived. When people think about you and your partner and feel a sense of unsolicited affection and respect, for each of you as individuals and for the quality of the partnership you have together, I would call that a sign of success.

Signs: Freedom

The way we generally think of "freedom" in relationships is that we leave each other alone and each do whatever we want, but this inevitably leads to insecurity, isolation, and disempowerment. What we are aiming for is spiritual freedom, an inner orientation of no boundaries, no existential knot at the core of our being. We open up to this dimension of freedom in ourselves and that freedom then becomes the space we share with our partners, and that others can experience with us.

Your relationship can be a transmitter, a contagious light, and a source of wholesomeness for others. Creating an environment where that depth of freedom is the natural resting

state takes work. It takes contemplation. And most of all, it takes letting go at a deep level of those points of tension where we feel that we are at odds with life. Spiritual liberation and alignment loosens those knots in a way that nothing else can. When we're expressing and amplifying that space in our relationship, our entire marriage becomes based on a higher ideal, bringing us together and keeping us together, mutually invested in a deeper purpose.

Signs: Curiosity

Awakening to the captivating process of development in an evolutionary context brings with it a certain freshness. You may have noticed changes in yourself as you've been reading, and working with the contemplations in this book. Some people, when they begin to engage in this kind of work, start to experience a broadening of their interests. A natural curiosity starts to rise up and that curiosity generates an up swell of excitement and care, a self-generating momentum. How can we go further together? How can we share it with others? This energetic enthusiasm to come together with other people and discuss the values we're intentionally tracking in our intimate relationship is what develops our own shared values and ethic. It's a beautiful thing to be consciously involved in creating this type of shared agreement— it's much needed in our culture and still all too rare.

Some couples who have been married more than twenty years discover something unexpectedly fresh when they internalize a process-oriented spirituality. Part of the thrill is the sense that we're not exploring just for our relationship but rather that our relationship is being explored so we can express different values in culture. The wonder of new insights emerging out of ground that's been tilled for many seasons brings renewed inspiration. No matter how long you've known someone or how close you are, the quality of authentic emergence can always be brought forth—the life process is in constant motion and we can direct and participate in it in a conscious way. A thirty-year relationship is still ever new. As familiar as you are, you can always touch on unbroken ground.

Signs: Freshness

Some time ago a woman who'd been married for only a year but had been pursuing this work with me for a number of years described a moving experience of the unfamiliarity of her new relationship while simultaneously feeling a profound ease with her husband. A sense of longevity in the relationship was there even without significant shared history. And both were looking forward to the years ahead, imagining how the tenor and hue of their patterns together might transform through familiarity and time.

This quality is fascinating because it occurs in a context of deepening familiarity and intimacy. The breadth of life experience that naturally results from our time together occurs in a liberated context that makes our intimacy ever new. You feel like you could be together for another forty years yet still maintain that quality of freshness, that sparkle, and the growth that comes from the eternal spring of a liberated ground. As we find a way to live that puts our attention on that which we don't already know, we do away with a veneer of over-familiarity that suffocates potentially good relationships. Centering in a liberated context where Spirit is first brings an immediate freshness into the relationship. Then your time with your partner doesn't become a stagnant pond. You've created and are continually re-creating a vibrant pool of new emergence.

Signs: Maturity

When couples practice a spiritually informed evolutionarily minded path in relationship, there are two things that paradoxically happen: we discover a freshness and newness, a familiarity and maturity. The quality of maturity is important. A primary function of this path is to help us express a maturity of self and a maturity in relationship to life. And this is not just a stability and reliability that comes from life experience but that comes from context, from prioritizing a rootedness in Spirit over the relentless flux of emotions.

Signs: Fearlessness

There's a certain type of anxiety that post-modernity breeds in our psyches. The more we become rooted in a spiritually awakened evolutionary worldview, the more that anxiety will diminish. Some of the signs of success couples have been thrilled to see emerge when they consciously embrace the context we've been speaking about is a sense of fearlessness, openness, and sensitivity. As the view opens up to allow the illumination from the deeper Self to flood our experience, we can handle tension without immediately becoming reactive, self-protective, shielded. We can choose when to respond and when to wait, based on respect, concern, and skillful means.

As we immerse ourselves in the spiritual dimension of Self, and as we learn to understand the dynamics of the different parts of the self work—the interplay of the ego and the psyche, the dynamics of Agape and Eros (the force that holds things together and allows integration and the force that generates new emergence) our evolutionary enthusiasm grows. Familiar fears recede into the background, becoming an ever-smaller part of our experience in life.

Driven by evolutionary enthusiasm and spiritual strength, we can slough off the fear of others and the fear of being seen as who we are. The more we allow ourselves to take root in these principles, the less that type of existential fear is going to hover in the forefront of our experience. We may still experience tension and we'll no doubt experience challenges. But something else more compelling is taking its place at the forefront of awareness. That something else is the already fullness of self and our always greater human potential.

One of the most important things we can do is to live and demonstrate an alternative possibility in which we're all ourselves—unique expressions of the spiritual process—sharing a perspective that fosters respect, space, affection, love, support, intimacy, trust, stability, and growth. There is no one way this should look. But there is a solid foundation with respect to context. If we can be clear about that and live from that and express its fruits, then we'll be able to offer something of incredible value to contemporary culture.

CONTEMPLATIONS

List three qualities you consider to be signs of success. Then list three additional qualities that will indicate a positive change in your own relationship.

_____

_____

_____

_____

_____

_____

_____

_____

_____

_____

_____

_____

_____

Reflect on the new aspects you want to bring into your engagement. Make some notes of several things you can do that will help bring about that depth.

_____

_____

_____

_____

_____

_____

_____

_____

_____

Spend some time this week on the web and explore other references to a few of the signs of success that we've discussed here. Note how words that you use to describe positive qualities can mean very different things. Reflect on some ways the meaning and associations that you find in other contemporary writing may be very different than the one that is beginning to open up in your experience.

Fullness: Discovering a Source of Completion

Where does our culture tell us to look for fulfillment in life? Is it from sex? Power? Prestige? Fame? Security? Purpose? Where do we look for fulfillment in our relationships? Is it from affirmation? Companionship? Security? Fun? Children? Shared mission? What are those moments when we feel most fulfilled?

As we open up these questions distinctions start to emerge in our experience. What becomes clear is that we are simply not always clear about what we are looking for, where we think we'll find it, or why we think it's important in the first place. And if we're not clear about what we're aiming for, it's very unlikely we'll hit any target, never mind hitting one dead center.

The question of fulfillment is fundamental both in our personal relationships and in our relationship to life. The best way to approach both is from the inside out, starting from the deepest place in oneself. It is here that we discover a source of Fullness that comes from insight into who we already are. It is here that we experience the immediacy of wholeness, peace, ease, release, happiness, stability, empathy, and Love. It is here that our existential angst dissolves. We let go of the feeling that something's wrong, that we're not in the right place, that we are missing something but we don't quite know what it is. We experience wholeness, fullness, and an infinitude of Self as ourselves. It is here that we experience completion at the very core of our being. It is here that we can take a stand in relationship to life upon an entirely different ground. And it is from this stand that we can fundamentally change how we relate to others.

This is a two-step process. The first is awakening to who we are at a level of Self. The second is contemplating what that awakening means, and how this awakening changes what we look for in life and what is truly important in our relationships.

But first things first: we need to awaken to who we are.

Spiritual and religious traditions illuminate different paths for awakening to Self or God. This realization is the time-honored heart of mystical practice and the path of enlightenment. One way to get a glimpse of this infinitude is through experiencing "no boundaries" in meditation. Another way to awaken to infinitude is through experiencing the quickening of the evolutionary current within oneself. Some insights of Gopi Krishna on the kundalini experience or Andrew Cohen's path of Evolutionary Enlightenment point to an awakening to the impulse of evolution surging through us as our own Self. Experiment with these awakenings; keep searching until you know, in your heart of hearts, that you have come home and have truly came in touch with a dimension of self that is always present, regardless of whether you are aware of it or not. This dyad—the Self absolute and the life impulse—underpins all of existence and animates all sentient beings. Peering beyond the veil of separate existence dissolves our sense of existential fear, of lack, and our loneliness, isolation, and inertia. The remedy, as spiritual masters have taught, lies not in a palliative administered by another but by ourselves awakening to the nature of existence.

When we discover this source of completion, inspiration, and "Love without end," how we come together with others, including with our spouses, changes in fundamental ways. We come together as already whole in ourselves. And when our spouses share this same realization of Self, together we are free to experience and experiment with a profound joy and fulfillment in many dimensions of life.

When we are full at this level of self, our aspiration to develop and change—to pursue ever-greater fulfillment in life—can become a positive tension. Areas that may have created friction between our partners and ourselves can become a source of creativity, animating and inspiring us to explore beyond our comfort zones, reach beyond self-imposed limitations. We can dare to believe in ourselves and to back up our beliefs with our own trustworthiness, strength, open-heartedness, and joy.

The desire to find fulfillment is human. It also challenges us to develop in new ways. When we put first things first and seek an ultimate source of fulfillment in and as ourselves then our coming together with another will be on a bedrock of existential ease and fullness, and that makes all the difference for what is possible between two human beings.

Let us flesh this out more in the section ahead.

5 FULFILLMENT

If you look up synonyms for fulfillment you find words like contentment, completion, success, and satiation. It calls to mind happiness, gratitude, and joy, being whole and complete, enriched and satisfied. We can all experience a more fulfilling, satisfying, and liberated relationship in our intimate partnerships, and through that we can express something attractive and stabilizing for our culture at large. It's a gift to everyone around us when we can fulfill these two aspirations—individual fulfillment and cultural change—through our relationship.

Many people experience moments of fulfillment but don't know necessarily what causes it, how they can deepen it, or what to do when it disappears. In this chapter, we're going to explore what the source of profound fulfillment is. When we can articulate, define, and locate the source of our inner satiation, we'll be able to pull it forward from the backgrounds of our lives, cultivate it, and make choices that align with it. As we do this with increasing skill, we start building a wholesome and powerful momentum in our lives.

Understandably, we want to experience fulfillment in our marriage; we want a sense of home and belonging, we want to love and be loved. And yet, many people experience some degree of angst or trepidation about our ability to ever fulfill our own longing for wholeness. Many of us harbor a not-so-secret conviction that true or lasting fulfillment may always be out of our reach.

A Source of Fulfillment: Contemporary Answers

Where does our culture point us to seek for fulfillment? Generally, the first things that come to mind are: work, family, power, sex, validation, financial success, material comfort, entertainment, and sometimes a higher calling. We're trained to equate fulfillment with stimulation. Physical and emotional excitement though are by nature transitory, ephemeral. Or, we are oriented to seek fulfillment from something outside ourselves—even beauty, nature, and intimate connections with others—are still found outside of ourselves. We rarely see ourselves as full, complete, and solid in ourselves. We're perpetually dependent on something or someone beyond ourselves to experience completion, peace, rest, and satiation. Can you see how, essentially, we are looking for fulfillment, as the country song goes, "in all the wrong places?"

We look for fulfillment in different places and from different levels of ourselves. Where we look for wholeness will affect our relationship with our partners. For example, if we're looking for fulfillment from material success and we don't achieve what we want, we can respond in our marriage with frustration or need—this is unnecessary and sets up an expectation that is impossible for our partner to remedy. We can start to get clearer about how this works by asking ourselves, what parts of ourselves are we fulfilling, in which way, and why? Are these pursuits valid and useful? Are they purposeful?

A Source of Fulfillment in An Endless Well

No one wants to be lonely and unloved, and many of us are afraid of feeling stuck, of passivity, and of a lack of inspiration overtaking us. What can address the root cause of our isolation, alienation, inertia, or dullness? The illumined ones point to a source of Love beyond the world; they recognize the world's gifts are fleeting. They point to a fulfillment that can withstand the test of time. And they speak of a source that could never be separate from us.

Spiritual illumination looks to the realization of a Self that is unchanging, to the realization of wholeness, unity consciousness, emptiness, and freedom. In the great traditions, we're pointed to a Self that is always fulfilled, always empty of any partialness, always complete in and of itself. That Self isn't dependent on being given anything. It isn't dependent on others. It's not dependent on anything else. It often arises unbidden, sneaking up on us from behind, enveloping us from within and without, taking us by surprise and bringing an overwhelming surety that at this level of ourselves, there never could be any lack because there is no other.

Those flashes of insight don't automatically bring order to our lives, they don't necessarily line our life up with the knowledge of fulfillment or completion. The reality of Oneness doesn't create order in and of itself, but it gives us a glimpse of a possibility, which we can begin to shape our values around. We don't have to have that experience all the time; our transformation rests in learning to recognize, trust, and value the intimation of a deep wholeness. We can then sculpt our lives in accordance with the truth it has revealed.

A rootedness in this "already fullness" engenders a fundamentally different order of relatedness. When we come together with another and express our love, affection, respect, partnership, and joy while resting in that which was never separate from either of us, a sacred consciousness permeates our relationship. We are inherently free of dependency on each other. The realization of this mystical source of fulfillment unseats the roots of neediness, loneliness, and mistrust that can so easily arise in relationship.

CONTEMPLATIONS

Bring the experience of a moment of fullness to mind, reflect on it, and identify different times you may have had a glimpse of a part of your experience that felt overflowing in and of itself. Make some notes of the qualities you experienced and what gave you intimations of a dimension of Self that was already complete.

_____

_____

_____

_____

_____

Now imagine what it might be like to come together with your partner from this knowing of "already fullness."

_____

_____

_____

A Source of Fulfillment in Shared Purpose

A sense of ongoing fulfillment or rootedness in ourselves also comes from defining our relationships according to our shared life's mission. We then work towards a common goal through collaborative efforts, regardless of what either of us may be struggling with at any given time.

I had the opportunity to meet President Jimmy Carter and his wife Rosalind at a little church in Plaines, Georgia. He was 89 years old at the time, and she around the same age. They've been together since he was 22. They are beautiful people, humble and engaged in life. What touched me about them is their open affection for each other and their partnership in a greater commitment. They share spiritual fellowship. They share a common vocation in life. They travel around the world, working to alleviate poverty and political unrest in Africa, South America, the Middle East. Obviously they have weathered many challenging times together, as would any leader who has occupied such a powerful and delicate position. But their relationship appears to be supported by their inner calling. Why do marriages like these uplift our hearts? The qualities of partnership, purpose, and direction lay strong plumb lines, bringing stability, intimacy, and resilience in the face of the winds of life.

A Source of Fulfillment in Perpetual Motion

We can also discover a source of fulfillment in the forward march of evolution, in the endless process of reaching towards the future. This propulsion and evolutionary momentum is what Teilhard de Chardin described as a pull on the present from the future potential of greater Love. Evolution is complicated and there are many complex and competing theories about the various organizing forces at play that enable higher orders of complexity to emerge and become new habits or possibilities in the world. Internalizing some of the broad principles of evolutionary theory can reframe our way of being together. Rather than seeking for an unattainable level of security, we can become one and at peace with a current of continuous movement, ebb and flux, tension and release. We realize process is not synonymous with lack; perpetual motion is the nature of all matter, energy, and life.

Let's look at a process image of how we came to be in the marriages we are currently in. Some cosmologists speak about how, at the very beginning of our universe, there was a point of infinitely hot, infinitely dense matter that exploded, spewing forth an instantly expanding time and space. That plasma then formed a sub-atomic "particle zoo," which, in turn, cohered into protons, neutrons, and electrons. Those, in turn, cohered into atoms and they cohered into molecules. The molecules aggregated into compounds and, through gravity, the compounds came together as stars, planets, and moons. Then in a fantastic coming together, hydrogen and oxygen formed into water and water helped create the conditions for life, which gave birth to the first life forms—single-celled organism. For two billion years they remained as they were but ultimately bonded together into the first multi-cellular creatures. It is from here that the plant and animal world exploded. As the conditions for emergence became more favorable and as the complexification of life gained in pace, the consciousness that arose evolved new capacities. Much further on down the evolutionary road those emergent capacities came to include human self-reflective consciousness—the capacity to objectify one's own thoughts.

Why does exploring the march of development from stardust to humans become relevant to our discussion about fulfillment in our marriages? It lays a foundation that reorients our touchstones in life. It links us with developmental principles that govern energy, matter, and sentience. These principles are the groundwater running through our individuated selves. They guide the development of our higher humanity and transcend our individual histories. As we learn to perceive life with fresh eyes, we awaken to a profoundly interrelated "meshwork" of forces. From here, we draw a knowledge and experience of fullness and completeness, at our core we recognize our inseparability with the vast, intricate, interconnected moving process. We as a single life may experience all kinds of needs and apparent lacks, but we, as inseparable with the current of evolution, are as full as the universe is full.

Discovering how to come together in deeper and deeper ways that express profound unity, subtle individuation and complexification, inseparable interrelatedness is part of our human purpose in life. It creates joy. The more we recognize the essential fullness and completeness of the process of evolution, then as we come together to create with another, whether we're coming together with our partners, we're in relationship out of the fullness and the creative explosion of the life process. We're not coming together out of lack. This is a powerful shift of identity. And when fulfillment meets fulfillment, the higher order of complexity that can emerge in our union is extraordinary.

Identifying new wells of fulfillment immediately impacts the way we see our partners and the way we value our time together. It brings forward the beauty of being a human being and of being conscious. It creates all kinds of space in which to work out interpersonal issues and questions. When we're already fulfilled, we are left with more energy for others and for evolution. We want the best not just for ourselves, we want the best period. That creates a powerfully wholesome environment together.

CONTEMPLATIONS

Reflect on these questions: How do you feel unfulfilled in certain ways and want to learn how to cultivate your connection with a more active sense of purpose and development? How do you feel fulfilled and want to understand better what creates the fulfillment you already feel?

_____

_____

_____

_____

_____

_____

_____

_____

_____

_____

Consider these sources of fulfillment. How do they contribute or detract from your experience of well-being in relationship?

- Power, money, position, influence
- Connectedness, affirmation, attention, recognition
- Co-creation, purpose, mission

_____

_____

_____

_____

_____

_____

_____

_____

_____

_____

_____

6 TRUST

In the last chapter, we spoke about finding a sense of wholeness in Spirit's inherent fullness so when we come together with our partners we come together as already complete, no longer lacking or in need. Sharing a desire to be together, our love for one another, and a creative aspiration to do something together is a very different starting point than coming together in order to fulfill each other.

People ask me, "If you're already full, why be in a relationship at all?" That points to a very deep inquiry: the relationship between the One and the Many, between the absolute nature of consciousness and the reality of our humanness, between that Spirit which we can't see and the beautiful multiplicity of the manifest world. Relatedness is the essence of the human heart. Our transformation occurs through perfecting our relatedness in Love, empathy, compassion, and higher development. The fact that more and more of us are contemplating the effect of enlightenment on our values in relationships is already a powerful catalyst for cultural change.

As we redefine how we come together using the lens of an evolutionary and spiritual perspective, our relationships become more satisfying and meaningful. This view is not designed to evolve us out of intimate relationships but rather to create a strong and resilient ground for intimacy. We build a foundation of mutual support, autonomy, unity, and transformation. We spend so much of our lives together, let's infuse our time with meaning and direction.

A Foundation of Trust

In this section, we are going to explore the foundation and nature of trust, introducing a way to think about trust and trustworthiness that can create a seamlessness and stability in your marriage. Webster's defines trust as "an assured reliance on the character, ability, strength or truth of something or someone." Trusting means we can rely on something. It means that we are sure that "something" will be there for us. Trust is foundational in an intimate relationship. We need to be sure that through life's instability, there are certain fundamentals in our relationship that are solid, that we can rely on so we have firm ground to support our inquiry into higher matters.

If we're aspiring to create something new as a couple, we're stepping into the unknown together and we're opening up at levels of ourselves that rarely get exercised. We're awaking to a positively-oriented but insecure context. That insecurity is one of evolutionary change. When our primary focus in life is on inner transformation for the purpose of outer, more collective change, we find ourselves compelled to explore new terrain and push ourselves beyond our limits. To do that, we want to be able to trust. We want to trust the path we're on, the context we're exploring, and our partners.

Unity of Purpose

In evolutionary and spiritual contexts, what we're committed to is an unfolding of our higher potentials. We're aspiring for a lasting and significant transformation of self, a purification of motive, smoothing out the rough edges so we're no longer acting in ways that are selfish and motivated by baser intentions. Ultimately we're committed to the evolution of the capacities of consciousness and the culture. Our personal commitment to purify ourselves at those levels of self is part of our spiritual commitment, and our integrity with respect to that commitment creates a strong foundation for our marriage.

When we're in a spiritual relationship, we support each other in our efforts to evolve. We support each other by giving each other room, space, and inspiration to develop. We allow each other to be and become our best; moreover, we expect it. We see our husband or wife through the lens of their higher potentials. We see possibility and strength first before we see limitations and lack. We're motivated by respect, joy, and love to help each other bring out those strengths. We share that purpose—the path of illumination and transformation—together.

When we share a genuine desire for each other's development, we're inspired to be a good example for our partners. We show them our best side because of the love and affection we share. Our relationships become the safest environment to dare to imagine ourselves as a human being with more weight and inner stature than we may have ever considered possible.

An ongoing conversation about higher purpose in life creates a field of trust. When I say "purpose" I don't only mean the purpose of our marriages but rather, life's purpose. What are we here for? What do we want to achieve with our precious human life? What impact do we want to have on culture? What legacy do we want to leave?

When we come together in a marriage to define our shared purpose, even if we've lived with our partners for many years, we will likely be amazed at what we discover. The more familiarity we have with each other, we can actually pursue spiritual depth and articulate our vocation, our higher calling, with more dimensionality.

A higher purpose springs from a fire within that compels us to reach beyond the known, to live a life that matters. When we hear each other express that fire, that mystery, that noble aspiration, it's moving and uplifting. Even if we have known each other for decades, exploring our deeper purpose, what Love in action can look like, is ever new. It draws us nearer to each other in a shared exploration of that which can never become old.

Engaging together about higher purpose fortifies the foundation of any relationship. "What do we want our lives to be about?" "What is human purpose?" We don't have to articulate the same understanding of Spirit as our partners. We may see different images of what that higher calling is. We may want to alter the nature of our relationship based on what we find out together. We may unearth more significant differences between us than we realized, or the opposite. In this spirit and context, we can work with any possibility that arises because we will be approaching difference from a ground of trust, from space and openness to new possibilities and ways of being together.

Unity of purpose and the viability and strength in our relationship depends on communication that is receptive, discerning, loving, and mature. How sensitive am I to creating space that is based in trust, that allows for change, development, and new insights that lead us to change the course we set in the past?

An evolutionary and spiritual context protects and preserves space for continual development and transformation while also protecting and preserving the Love and respect in the field created between our partners and ourselves. It establishes trust in that which is at its core, always a mystery. It also establishes our commitment to that same inner light that has illumined consciousness throughout the ages.

The Art of Communication

Some of us may be with partners who share the exact evolutionary context that we do, and some of us may be with partners who pursue a different spiritual path. The latter is not necessarily an obstacle, as long as the expectations are clear and there is mutual respect and support for each other's rhythm of development. We don't need to impose our paths on each other, but rather support each other's flowering. Can we be this open and trusting, while maintaining a positive tension that calls out the best from each one of us?

What happens when our expectations are different? Maybe your partner says "I'm committed to the same thing you are," but you each see your own higher purpose very differently. Communication is essential. Communication in a spacious environment encourages growth. But you have to be courageous and sensitive. If you care for each other enough to be in a sexual relationship together—you respect each other, are attracted to each other, and want to live together as partners—one expression of that care is abiding trust in each other's true heart and spiritual sensitivity. That trust will create enough space to have transparent and open communication about the ways we interpret the higher contexts in our lives.

And if we still differ? Then we'll need to find out if that difference is indeed an obstacle to continuing to be in an intimate relationship with each other, or if it's a difference that we can work with, use to move forward toward our higher purpose. We can come to a genuine understanding, or an appreciation of our differences, and decide what it means about our relationship, all the while never betraying our love for each other. The more we are rooted in a fullness of self, and the more we don't require our spouses to be a particular way in order for us to feel our own inherent and existential completion, the easier we will be able to navigate the differences between us, while fostering creativity and development.

A common situation that can create the experience of disrupted trust is falsely assuming mutual understanding. The more time we live together, the easier it is to assume shared views. Communication is an art. We need to work to cultivate our ability to be present, to seek to understand with new ears, new eyes, and an open heart at every moment. This may sound simple but putting this into practice requires commitment to inner transformation and follow through with the inner work required. Our more refined skills in communication come from placing emphasis on the quality of consciousness we share more than on either of our personal views or issues. Establishing a field around us that's supportive, clear, open, unobstructed, and reliable takes sensitivity, objectivity, and an ease with a mystery we cannot understand.

Commitments

To develop, we want our relationship to be built on solid ground. We want to establish wholesome boundaries and expectations, take our time to get to know each other so that the agreements we come to are really the natural articulation of the quality of our relationship that is already there.

There are certain fears or concerns that we want to make obsolete. There are conditions for trust to set together and keep alive. Then when friction arises between us, we deal with the issues. We don't unearth the foundation beneath our feet. We all have blind spots. We all need to develop. We do things that unintentionally upset our loved ones. But these things can be dealt with in a context of fundamental trust. When we establish shared agreements or boundaries, we build a framework of respect. And we set structures in place to respond with dignity if those boundaries are transgressed. A question that regularly arises in explorations around trust in relationships has to do with commitment—and broken commitments. There are different levels of commitment. One area that can cause needless friction is if someone commits to something relatively insignificant and then doesn't follow through because something objectively more important arose. Does that break trust? Is it a sign of more fundamental unreliability? How do you discern the difference?

Bigger life issues come up sometimes and push smaller tasks to the background. That's not a capital offense. But the motive to overcommit creates an impression of unreliability. Let the focal point for change be here—on the level of motive. When the motive is to be reliable and trustworthy, our communication will become more straightforward.

Not propelled by needing to please or by an appearance of being willing, we'll express what we mean without over commitment.

Triggers

Why don't people trust in a relationship? Common rationales include: "My partner is unpredictable," "He or she doesn't follow through," "I never know what to expect." "I don't know if my partner wants what I do," "My husband or wife isn't there for me; they don't meet my needs." "We aren't open with each other. We don't really say what we mean." "I don't know if my partner's faithful to me."

Do you recognize any of these? Dynamics like these may be present in our lives now or have been at one time. Some of these seeds of disharmony can be addressed through simple and direct communication and don't need to create mistrust. Clear communication means being able to speak together with a mutual desire to understand how we're influencing each other and find out whether our ideals may differ in some fundamental ways. We may see things differently, that's fine. We can learn from these differences together. When we're not seeing the same thing and we're not able to talk about it, it creates shadow. And shadow creates unnecessary mistrust.

There are seeds of disharmony that fall outside of the bounds of our shared agreements. If that is the case, we may need to make changes, respecting first and foremost ourselves and the good reasons we came together with our spouses in the first place, all that's been accomplished together, and the higher purpose of human life.

Courage

Culture is created through our interactions, through the guidelines we set in our relationships with each other. When we aspire to create a culture that expresses something higher than the fragmentation and alienation that we too often experience, we live from a different position. We're no longer waiting for the world to be trustworthy, we're not sitting back with our arms folded across our chest and looking out at the world saying, "prove to me that you're trustworthy, and then I'll trust." Instead, we have taken ownership and leadership in our lives; we've embraced the responsibility of becoming trustworthy ourselves. Becoming trustworthy ourselves is simple and enormously challenging. We develop integrity of word and deed. We are true to our higher ideals. We live a life of respect, dignity, and authenticity. No longer victim to circumstances around us, we take hold of the reins of our own lives. We take initiative to become moral people, aligned with our higher values and life aspiration.

Regardless of whether we have been consistent and reliable individuals in the past, once we choose to be trustworthy, we can become well integrated individuals. In that alignment, we demonstrate that human beings can change—that we can transform ourselves through intention and effort. Then we pave the way for others to trust. We express stability through our own humility and transparency. This is a powerfully independent position—which takes courage and care to live from—and it inspires others to follow suit with their own transformation.

It can be challenging to stay steady when emotions are heated, when we feel angry (even justifiably so). Can we respond from a position that expresses a fundamental trust in life? Can we respond in a way that expresses our desire to be as mature and open as possible, expecting much more from ourselves than just holding our temper? Can we imagine a higher capacity in ourselves and call ourselves to live from a deeper place, not just a little bit deeper, but much deeper and become real live example of what's possible? That is the ground of trust. That is the trust we are called to embody

when we aspire to be exemplars on an evolutionary spiritual path.

Humility

Humility in the face of what we don't know creates trust. When we come together with a purpose as big as the evolution of consciousness and culture, then, of course, there's going to be a tremendous amount that we don't see and we don't know. As we grow and develop through our lives, sometimes we'll be in a flow, everything will feel effortless, and sometimes we'll have to make enormous effort. Of course we all have fears. Sometimes we're afraid of change. Sometimes we're afraid of people. Sometimes we're afraid that we've made a mistake, and maybe we have. We have to own our fears. We have to own our arrogance. We have to own our insecurities. Having humility, or transparency, in the face of our shortcomings, creates stable ground. When we're on stable ground, we'll be able to sort out confusion as it arises.

We want to avoid imposing our own confusion on another. We don't want to say things that are challenging for another and then realize that we were wrong. It's better to sort through our own confusion as much as possible and we come to a place of more solid trust. Some people realize clarity and space through meditation, others through contemplation, others in discussion with friends. Humility is a care as well as a recognition of human fragility. Living from a posture of humility creates a field of flexibility and trust that we all long to live in.

Space

Giving each other space to develop and giving charged situations some time before we draw too many conclusions strengthens the trust between us. The simplicity of allowing some space, cooling the engines of emotion, goes a long way. Not only do we not react out of habit and impulse, but we also put into action our trust in our partners' intentions. We're all human, we all make mistakes, we all interpret things narrowly. Space is the expression of trust in action.

How do we "remember" to leave space? Being anchored in shared purpose gives us access to emotional stability and maturity. We're more aligned and identified with the greater life mission we share with our partners than with a particular flare up, so we protect the field of consciousness between us. We keep it clear of emotionality and static.

Respect

Trust gets built in relationships when we don't assume an over-familiarity with each other—when we recognize that there is that mysterious spiritual fire in each and every human being. As well as we can know each other, there's always going to be an unexpected unfolding, and that's the beautiful thing about the diversity of human beings.

In an evolutionary context, even if we have been together twenty, thirty, or fifty years, we want to support our creative unfolding so that we don't have to feel, think, or even believe the same thing all the time. We don't interpret everything the same way—a healthy diversity exists between all of us, a diversity that doesn't have to inhibit intimacy. Diversity can instead bring richness and relief; we don't want to be the same human being.

CONTEMPLATIONS

In this chapter's contemplations, focus your thoughts and make your values more conscious and explicit. Consider these questions:

What is your purpose?

_____

_____

_____

_____

_____

What is the purpose of your relationship?

_____

_____

_____

_____

Are you living and relating to your partner in a way that expresses that purpose?

Could you be living and relating more intentionally? Could you explore your shared purpose more—or more constructively—together?

_____

_____

_____

_____

_____

Reflect on trust and on what we've covered. List three ways you can go about things differently to alleviate feelings of mistrust.

_____

_____

_____

_____

_____

_____

_____

_____

_____

Take some time to contemplate your relationship. In the dynamic between you and your partner, where and how do you experience a spiritually informed, evolutionary context for trust? Where do you feel you and your spouse get caught in unnecessary scenarios that leave a residue of mistrust? What are the actual disagreements about your shared context that, in your opinion, need further questioning and work? Make note of your reflections.

Trust, Purpose & Cultural Evolution

When I went searching for inspiring quotes about trust for this chapter, I stumbled across a variety of reflections from visionary thinkers to sources in popular culture that made me think. One of my all time favorite American philosophers and commentators on life, Ralph Waldo Emerson advised, "Trust men and they will be true to you; treat them greatly and they will show themselves great." On the other end of the spectrum, a pop relationship site declared, "Trust issues can crop up out of nowhere especially when an attractive new friend or secrecy enters the romance." Let's face it, pop culture has a pretty jaded lens on this area of life. In my cursory searches, there were unbelievably few insightful reflections on trust. And most of what I found encourages us to claim the freedom to indulge in emotional states and limit our expectations in relationship.

I started to reflect more on trust and how potentially culture-changing it is. The idea that deep and lasting trust in romantic relationships comes from sharing a higher purpose hardly sounds like the stuff of cultural revolution. Revolution is overthrow, new order, upheaval. Greater rights. Greater freedoms. Greater innovation. Trust based on sharing a higher purpose together sounds, well, tame. But think about it: If our higher purpose is to facilitate inner transformation and the emergence of new orders of relatedness and our commitment is to perpetual growth and development, a bedrock of trust is essential. Building a framework in our marriages that is based on a shared commitment to developing spiritually establishes a very different status quo. Consider how your own sense of trust immediately deepens when you create a context as big as evolution for your relationship. Trust takes root when you then commit to that context and share that mission with your partner. Experience how much joy, peace, stability, security, respect, and Love immediately starts to well up in your consciousness. Then you can see how this perspective really has the potential to make up a new social order.

I live in Philadelphia, and when I go for walks in the morning down sun-dappled cobblestone streets, I keep my eye out for the historical markers that line the pavement or are fixed in transparent sheets to the windows of many houses. I live right in the neighborhood where early abolitionists, signers of the American Declaration of Independence, and freedom fighters walked and lived a couple hundred years ago. I love it because it impresses on me how lasting shifts in history were made by people like us, who in their culture and time stood for larger ideals—and lived that dream together with others.

Imagine in 200 years time simple placards marking the homes where early adopters of this process perspective lived. Individuals like us, who embodied the courage to see beyond contemporary culture's values, and who endeavored to live, in their most intimate relationships, according to a new and higher vision of what's possible. In that creed, trust is a cornerstone of relationships—trust based on a mutual commitment to perpetual development and higher emergence. Now imagine that we really were successful. This shift of values took hold in just enough individuals and became viable, the new status quo, for culture at large. That would truly be a mark in history.

7 HOME

After a certain age, when we hear the word home, it doesn't conjure up our parent's house anymore. It's something we expect to create in our marriage; we expect to experience coming home when we are with each other. Think about it though, we're not necessarily very clear about what we're looking for, why we're looking for it, whether what we're looking for is actually the right thing to look for, or if it's even valuable at this point in time. There's so much fluidity and change. Is the idea of home an outdated one, a notion from the past that no longer applies? The arts, in particular movies and television are useful to study because we're all influenced by popular culture, and popular culture also parodies and delivers the values we hold.

Broadly accepted images of home change as culture changes. Remember the classic musical Fiddler on the Roof and the sense of home—and transition—that tale conveys? The story begins with a traditional home where the Papa did one thing, the Mama did another, and the daughters fit into that structure. A specific set of orders and rules sustained the consciousness of that home. The family unit was tightly set inside a community. As the plot unfolds, the world is in a state of transition. First their home as a physical dwelling was disrupted and the values that created home also got displaced. Safety, security, faith, relationships all experienced upheaval. Home transitioned from a way of life and community what you could see, touch, and rely on to internal bonds. It's powerful to consider that depth of transition and the factors at play.

TV shows like Leave It to Beaver illustrate modern values in 1950s America. The mother and father in their starched and beautiful clothes lived in a tidy house, with nice-looking children. Mother baked cupcakes and was always at home. Father went off to work in the morning and kept an ordered and loving discipline in the house. How many of those values still hang like dusty cobwebs in the back of our minds, seemingly outdated yet still present, brushing our consciousness with a light but discernible touch?

As we moved into the 1960s, we started to see different family units. We started out with The Brady Bunch, single parents who were widowers each with three children. We also started to see more edgy family units: Marlo Thomas in That Girl was the first prime-time television, female character who was not married, who had both a boyfriend and a career and was not looking to create a traditional home. This was radical at the time. As we ventured into the 1980s, we had Will & Grace, young, postmodern friends creating a home together but with no romantic relationship between them.

Our images of the family structure have certainly transformed, but a lot of what we hold as an ideal is still measured off of values that come out of times or lifestyles that are not our own.

In your relationship, what is home? What would you consider home to be? What are some images that represent home?

When I ask this question of couples, they tend to express some interesting qualities. They describe "home" as the rhythms of living together; ease and harmony; a consciousness that comes from oneself and also a space or place we can enter into; a place of support and safety; a place whose inhabitants speak the same language.

Home represents that place we associate with love. It signifies family, acceptance, being at one with ourselves and our values. Many people are already working quite hard to establish a different set of values to define home in the new century, and yet they also want the stability that was so present in the more traditional culture we know of from the past. How do we create a wholesome environment that is safe, secure, and stable yet not a throwback to a different period of time with values that don't align with our current, higher aspirations?

In order to create these new values, we have to be able to articulate them. We have to put in effort to bring them forth, pulling them from the imaginal into the present, otherwise we default into what we know, habits and values we grew up with.

Home in Process

The way I see it, home is best seen as qualities of consciousness. It points to a type of Love, a way of coming together with others that wants what is best overall, that perpetually supports and brings us forward for the sake of our higher development. It's a love that demands that we rise up, and allows us the space and freedom to discover new entry ways towards development. Home is alignment with our most significant realizations and highest aspirations.

This consciousness that we can come to identify as home, that joy and stability, comes from being at rest in ourselves, from realizing that dimension of Self that cannot be taken away from us, no matter how many disappointments we go through, and no matter how many challenging times we have to face.

When we think back to that last scene of Fiddler on the Roof, the characters ousted from their home through political unrest, there are many challenging situations that can separate us from our own physical homes, from our families, from those we love and cherish the most. These traumas are real and happen to far too many of us around the world still. Yet, we can discover a place to rest that is constant even while the very real turmoil of the world goes on about us. It takes strength of character to abide here, but we can develop the spiritual strength to do so, and when we do, no matter where we are, we will embody that love and will transmit that experience of finding home in our mystic heart to others.

Home in an evolutionary context comes with an underlying paradox, the polarity of awakening to Self and simultaneously to process. This consciousness of home transmits rest, peace, love, safety, trust, and, simultaneously, a call, a challenge, a pull to reach beyond the known, to participate more fully in life. Embodying that paradox creates an environment at home that gives us rest and succor from the troubles of the world. It inspires us to become more than we are and to contribute our own expression of perpetual development to the world. Deeply fulfilled, we transmit peace to others; awake and inspired, we spark curiosity and exploration.

The more intimate we are with that part of ourselves, the more we will respect those qualities of consciousness, and the easier time we will have creating an environment that safeguards that space. We instinctively won't act in ways that disturb the field of consciousness around us. We won't let ourselves get angry about things we that are not that significant. We won't want to create static in our environment by being disrespectful to our spouses. We'll respond instead to that which fosters a joy, ease, and affection at home.

A variety of religious traditions talk about home being a place where strangers are always welcome. You can see that stability, higher consciousness, generosity of spirit, and humanity as something that we create with those we are intimate with. We create it not just for ourselves but also for everyone else.

Rhythm & Ritual

The movements that create home with our partners are a dance and ritual of contemplation, little traditions that recollect why we're together and clarify what we want to accomplish. Many of the religious structures seek to elevate consciousness by establishing rhythms in the home, around meals, or times and occasions for prayer. Those rituals give structure to life, reminding us of the bigger context for our lives. Are there tangible ways to bring that sanctification of life patterns back into our routines? Sitting down together when we eat, making our environment just a little more beautiful expresses a care for the consciousness of our homes, a love that extends to any who enter that space. When you take time to do these things together you might find that it has some surprising results. It may bring much more to the forefront of your relationship than you expect. You might not think such simple acts can make as big a difference as they do. That's where intention and consciousness come into play.

Have you consciously set a time or space for spiritual practice, contemplation, or inquiry? Setting certain times of contemplation together establishes our intentionality, we plant a stake in the ground of our busy lives that says, "here lives Spirit." Joy arises from this type of discipline, from creating more space for the inner. We may choose to practice alone or with our partner, both have their own strengths. Experiment with it. Experiment with the time you dedicate. Make it reasonable, but make it intentional.

Engaging with inner or numinous currents changes our relationship to home. It can alter how we perceive our living space, how we feel in that space, and even how we want to arrange it or what we want to do in our environment. Intentional actions that support our higher aspirations change our experience in the home we're building with our partner, and our relationship to our future together. Small frictions that arise between couples fall away. We are often able to rise above negative dynamics when something more delicate and real emerges in our experience. It also changes what others feel when they walk into our home. Our guests feel the peace, space, intentionality, and respect for the sacred.

Renunciation & Freedom

Home becomes a space that both expresses that freedom and invites you to re-awaken to and become intimate with inner liberation over and over again. Manifesting that in our relationships takes work. It won't necessarily come on its own.

When we were growing up, we probably had all kinds of rules that set boundaries for respect in the home . . . no phone calls during dinner, no reading at the table, no feet on the furniture, and all the other guidelines that established order and boundaries. We've grown. Still, boundaries define what occurs within them. What are the wholesome boundaries that create the consciousness we call home?

Discipline and renunciation, both inner and outer, are supportive, especially when defined along developmental lines. Renunciation of our lower impulses, our selfishness, narcissism, projections, neediness, our desire to use our partners to fulfill ourselves. Motives like these disrupt the consciousness of home. They create static in the environment and make it harder to keep our sights on our higher potentials. Inner discipline of our baser instincts creates self respect, a gentleness of spirit, and ease towards ourselves, our partners, and in the consciousness we create around us. The Rhythms of life

How we interact with each other can take perpetual refinement. We have different habits, and we may like to relate differently. When we start living together, there can be a steep learning curve to become sensitive and not personal about each other's rhythms. The rhythm of our life together is going to look different in our first year and sixtieth year of being together. Explore these patterns together, not just how you want the home rhythm to look, but why, then you'll be able to come together about your deeper intention in a way that's rich and supportive.

One woman I worked with described how she learned to create a more warm environment by giving her partner space when they both came back from work. As much as they loved to be together, home is also where we need to be able to decompress on our own and that's all right. It's not necessarily a sign of distance, or negative freedom, it can be a healthy aspect of our life rhythm.

The Aesthetic of Home

Our physical surroundings, as we've discussed, are important. Is the way we've organized our home inviting? Does it provide a welcoming space to contemplate, to be together and explore the edges of consciousness as well as the structures that enable us to develop? That's why in some of the Buddhist meditation environments, they create so much structure and simplicity in the space. Their aesthetic is central to their practice; it mirrors the qualities they're trying to attain in consciousness.

We want to continually create beauty, define new spaces and new structures that are more representative of a level of care that reflects our ideals and love of life. That care is ultimately a spiritual care, expressed towards our partners, towards those who walk into our home. It's a care for our higher ideal of bringing into being an awakened culture.

Both our inner and outer dwellings require spring cleaning. Often people easily relate to this level of intentionally refreshing their home, getting rid of the extraneous ideas or objects we accumulate but don't need any longer. Physically and psychically clearing out dead space makes room for new growth and for fullness and care to flood in. If our home represents a lot of bad habits of mind, and we've moved beyond those bad habits of mind, then it is good to make some changes to clear out things that represent negative patterns for us or represent times with our partners that we've evolved beyond.

The exploration of home can become profoundly anchoring. It can eliminate dichotomy between our spiritual lives and our "regular" lives. It can realign our most intimate relationship with the whole point of our deeper calling. Our home can become a refuge and center for prayer, a beacon of what's possible in culture, and a crucible for higher development.

CONTEMPLATIONS

Make a commitment to spend some time this week asking these questions of yourself. Set some time aside to speak about them with your partner.

_____

_____

In your relationship, what represents "home"? Is there a more subtle and nuanced way to think about those qualities?

_____

_____

_____

_____

_____

_____

_____

What could you do to make the house you currently live in more of a home? What could you do to bring more wholesome qualities of consciousness to the fore? Put emphasis on those qualities that you want others to experience and that build the culture you want to bring into being.

_____

_____

_____

_____

_____

_____

_____

What could you do with your partner that would bring those qualities of home to the forefront? Spend some time doing these activities.

_____

_____

_____

_____

_____

_____

_____

_____

_____

For a fun and instructive exercise, spend time searching YouTube for short videos, TV vignettes, or songs that express home. They don't necessarily have to illustrate the home that you believe in, but some quality or relationship to home. Notice the different images of home over time. Then think about where we are heading in the future. What qualities do you want to bring into being? What qualities create the best conditions for new capacities and insights to emerge? Look at both and take some time to think intentionally about what the home you want to create.

_____

_____

_____

_____

_____

Home . . . The Place We Return To

When we think about "home," we conjure up images that are an extension of our early home—that protected space in our mother's womb. Home, where we were held close, cared for, nourished, protected. As we mature, we begin to consciously create "home" for ourselves and for those around us. We gain control over our environment and shape the ambiance, the physical space, the emotional quality, the dos and don'ts allowed in what we now call home.

When we first leave our parent's home, some of us embark on a journey, we travel, we explore. On the road, home becomes what you can stuff into a rucksack. You transform into a perpetual guest and visitor, witness and observer in other's homes, a student of different values, cultures, and family units. A nomad. An outsider. At times we are self-sufficient, at others longing for a country, a family, a home to belong to, in search of a purpose that would put to rest that inner desire to belong.

College-age students, or recent graduates, often post-pone creating a home in that transient phase of their lives. Oblivious to the qualities of their physical surroundings, free flowing, distracted by external social networks, or consumed by the demands of a rigorous higher education program, it is often too early to consciously create the structures of home. University may become a time to experiment with utopian homes, with collective settings based on ideals. Even then, home often still points to the house they grew up in, where their parents are, where their now-empty bedrooms still hold the stuff of their childhood. And when that room becomes converted to a new study or game room or guest room, in spite of having gone unused for months or years, many young adults still describe an irrational sadness, a shadow of aloneness having been nudged out of the nest, feeling that something important has been taken away. Many feel, unexpectedly, in an in-between state, not knowing where to turn to for home. As the modern, nuclear family unit has become increasingly fluid, home has become, for more and more children, a transient experience. Shuffled from one parent to the other, sharing space with step-siblings for a period of time, the family configuration looks more like a wispy meshwork of connections. Economic challenges, both significant and insignificant, influence the physical home and often affect our underlying sense of stability and love more than is necessary.

Regardless of which vignette comes to mind first when we think of home, in each of these life moments, if we look more closely, we can see that home is not just associated with physical surroundings or specific people. It is associated with emotions and qualities of consciousness.

In an evolutionary spiritual context, we are looking at creating home—and a physical space—as an integrated expression of our most profound inner knowing. Regardless of who inhabits the space with us, how much financial affluence we are experiencing or not, where that home may be located, it is imbued with the qualities that nurture our spirit and foster development— Love, stability, respect, support, creativity, space, trust, aspiration, reverence.

Being at home in oneself is a powerful realization. When we rest in our Self a restless wanderlust dissolves. A desperate looking out at others who appear to have the ultimate "happy home" no longer plagues us. A sense that we are in the right place at the right time becomes our inner position.

Once we've discovered that home we experience rest, peace, and Love. We realize an anchor, a touchstone, we can always return to. If we go far enough with this, it becomes our identity, our reference point as self. In truth, it is a home we can't leave or be distant from because it is our own self. We may experience challenge, frustration, dissolution of one situation and transition into a new living situation. We may have times of struggle and times of ease. But fundamentally, when we realize that fullness of Self, we no longer need to look for "home" outside ourselves, searching for someone or someplace to fulfill us.

From that position of fullness, we now consciously build that consciousness with our partners, a home that best serves the emergence of new potentials. We weave an environment of love and stability, one that invites and inspires inquiry. One that makes conscious the dynamics between us and removes the ones that create unwholesome static and tension between people. We cultivate a field that supports each other's development, recognizing that we all have higher potentials that have yet to emerge. And we create an environment that makes others feel at home, where someone can walk through our door any time and experience that field of consciousness that expresses a Love for humanity and all the qualities that we associate with the most positive notion of home.

8 BALANCE

When we decide to approach our lives and our relationships in the context of a spiritually awakened evolutionary worldview, a variety of questions may arise: How do we join with our spouses and build a loving home and uplifting environment, while maintaining our own autonomy and space? How do we think about what we're doing in a way that is both pragmatic and connected to the multidimensional reality of our lives and also vast enough to give credit to the mysterious part of ourselves that aspires to become far greater human beings than we currently are? Can we, through our transformed humanity, shine as pillars of light in our contemporary culture?

Establishing habits in this new context may feel uncomfortable at first. They may open up space that is a little disconcerting, as well as illuminate interior closets that are overstuffed with ill-fitting, ill-fashioned ideas and beliefs. These areas need to be cleared out to make room for what is vibrant and new.

Most importantly, however, we are cultivating an awareness of our personal lives—how we live in marriage—as a central structure of culture. Intimate relationships are one of the pillars that reveal the values we hold collectively. These values shape us in ways we may not even be aware of. With heightened awareness, and spiritual sensitivities, we have an opportunity to fill out the intimacy, support, and love we experience with our partners, and also become an example of a different order of priorities in the culture at large, one that values respect, Spirit, growth, and ascension.

Working with Polarity

Transformation comes from being able to balance the two poles of change and stability. Balance is an art and a science of the heart, mind, and spirit. It's both intuitive and a skill we develop through experience, trial and error, insight from transformational paths and models, and most of all, from our own self-knowledge and integration of our life experience.

Developing a mature understanding of the dynamics at play in human transformation requires tremendous sensitivity and experience. Our maturation is marked by how skillfully we are able to adjust the tension between the two ends of the spectrum. Incubation and stability, and urgency and change are opposite poles on the continuum of transformation. We need stability and we need growth. The ratio is fluid; our needs move between the two poles. Balance occurs when growth and stability are in relationship with each other, in an intentional ebb and flow.

An Evolutionary Aspiration

In the social and spiritual culture we're creating, our aim is to establish an evolutionary dynamic that continually refreshes us and leads to a new depth of interaction and complexity of engagement. That's what Teilhard de Chardin pointed to in his writings, ever-higher orders of harmony and integration, more complex interaction and more intimate expressions of Love. But how do we get there?

Growth is necessary in relationships. Our individual growth is important, and for those of us who embrace an evolutionary worldview, we vest our personal growth with cultural significance. When inner growth has cultural significance, our development is an advancement or response to the patterns and mores of the generations before us. If our lives monotonously repeat the level of consciousness of our parents' generation, or their parents' generation, or ten generations before that, we found ourselves trapped in what Buddhism refers to as the wheel of endless becoming, where we endlessly cycle through birth to death, birth to death, birth to death, with no significant development. Human consciousness is capable of much more, but we have to push into the edges of growth—the possible calls on us to bear discomfort, to be flexible with change.

Change & Stability

Change is wholesome, an essential mark of evolutionary development and spiritual transformation. When asked whether change or stability is more important, many people express a strong bias for growth. I wholeheartedly agree, but with a caveat. When we're committed to evolve, we're committed to change, to becoming better individuals than we are now. But change without stability creates chaos. It creates pathologies, like cells that grow out of control and become a kind of cancer. Stability allows for integration, alignment, gestation, formation. But, stability without change is suffocating. Too much stasis leads to entropy.

Let's look at it in a little more detail. Creativity and growth create a positive momentum; inactivity creates a staleness, suffocation, negativity, small-heartedness, small-mindedness. People who don't change tend to be negative and inflexible. Their world shrinks. And once inertia sets in, it's hard to move out of it; it has its own gravity. At the same time, too little stability keeps us on edge in a negative sense. We're always a little wired, a little unsettled, a little out of sorts, and that often leads to erraticism and emotionalism. While inertia is stifling, sometimes we need space to gestate. Just like the earth has its fallow times to give the best yield, we need to be still, rejuvenate, and develop the sensitivity to listen from a different part of ourselves.

Couples have trouble because either there's not enough room for growth in the relationship or there's unsettling insecurity from too much change and not enough stability. Then we become so consumed managing change that we can't relax, let go, and let ourselves "come home" because we're so on edge. Change doesn't mean erraticism. Change means that we're willing to be flexible, lean forward, take risks, and experiment with new potentials.

When we care about evolutionary development, the intentionality of our lives and our values become even more important—not rigidity, but consistency of self at our core. Steadiness of purpose, values, vision, and affection are all ingredients for positive change to emerge. Stability creates a

trustworthy environment in which to embark on positive upheaval and change.

When you're in a context where the overriding value is evolutionary emergence, and your friendships and spiritual relationships bias the thrust of the evolutionary impulse, you'll find you don't need more upheaval in your marriage. You'll find it important for your own character development to balance that momentum with stability in your romantic relationship.

This balance between growth and consistency is an endlessly interesting dance. Like light skipping across the surface of a country lake, the rhythms are mercurial, doubling back on themselves, shifting direction. We want to hold these poles loosely, so we can be flexible and resilient, trusting and curious, able to experiment and equally able to hold our ground. Working these polarities calls on us to come together in our higher aspiration of inner growth while being true to our own developmental pace. That's an art—and a powerful expression of love.

Pacing

This is a common occurrence in marriages: one person wants the other to grow in a particular way at a particular time according to their prescription of how it should be. This can sometimes have positive results on development if an individual is sensitive and insightful, but it can be equally disruptive. Our evolutionary unfolding is a mystery and will occur in miraculous unexpected ways if we leave it room to do so.

When you were a child, did your science teacher ever show the class how plants sprout from seeds? Usually they took lima beans, put them in a wet paper towel against the side of a glass jar so you could keep them moist and watch them grow. What a miracle it is when a little tail of a shoot breaks through the bean! Imagine a young child, excited and impatient for their little seedling to grow faster. In a burst of enthusiasm, they reach in to the jar and grab the little bean with its emergent sprout. One tug to stretch it, help it grow a little faster. And then ... this budding botanist ends up with a tiny shoot in one small hand and a lima bean clutched in the other. We're not quite as fragile as a newly sprouted plant, but our consciousness is. Humility in the face of the development process goes a long way.

Managing Rhythms of Change & Integration

Part of the tension that can occur in a relationship is when one person is going through a period of intense growth and their partner is in a period of assimilation or integration. We don't always stay in the same rhythm of development together. That's okay. Successfully managing these poles means we have become more mature about each of our individuation processes and the differences between us. Allowing differences to be what they are and creating a home environment that supports both individuals in their independent rhythms maximizes what's possible between two people who care about each other and care about transformation.

At times, you and your partner may seem to be at odds. Listen carefully, and be sure to interpret your competing rhythms accurately. Just because one person is not going through a period of fireworks and growth spurts doesn't mean they're not developing. It might mean that they aren't, but it doesn't necessarily mean that. At times when our rhythms are out of sync, then we talk about it. When we articulate what's happening, we can better understand these dynamics and give each other the space or push each needs. What in our rhythms with each other is wholesome? What has become stale? How can we work together differently? By working to understand these polarities, we also hone our ability to work together, a process that creates true intimacy. Sharing our development together in this way, we form bonds and successes that make us closer.

The better we understand how human beings develop—the less likely we are to damage each other, like in the example of the child and the bean sprout. Over-enthusiasm, an overemphasis on growth, or unskillful pressure on areas of resistance, can squelch or stress a healthy developmental process. When we mature in our understanding of the complexities of human nature and consciousness we are in a position to facilitate the process of conscious evolution. And we can do this in our relationships because we've generated trust and intimacy between us. We can allow ourselves to explore these things not only to make our relationship better—which it will—but also to become cultural-change pioneers. The world needs more people who are mature about human development and able to navigate it with real skill, sensitivity, and compassion.

As we learn how to work this in our home environment, we bring that knowledge and sensitivity with us wherever we are, into all our relationships, into our workplace, our schools, our congregations of worship, wherever we may be in the shared environment of our culture. We need more of this awakeness in our world.

CONTEMPLATIONS

Describe the aspects of your relationship that are constant.

_____

_____

_____

_____

_____

_____

_____

_____

_____

_____

_____

_____

Describe the aspects of your relationship that are changing.

_____

_____

_____

_____

_____

_____

_____

List several habits that are old and need to loosen up and change. Why do they need to change? What are you trying to achieve?

_____

_____

_____

_____

_____

List several aspects of your relationship that express flux and that would be better off stabilizing. What would more consistency serve?

Think about a specific situation or dynamic in your relationship that you can approach differently. Make a commitment to actively work and explore the balance between change and stability in this area. Make some notes of how it is now and of the quality between you and your partner. Revisit this in a week and again in a month, and make some notes of how you've developed flexibility and a more conscious relationship to these two poles.

_____

_____

_____

_____

_____

_____

_____

_____

_____

_____

_____

_____

Balance . . . Working the Polarities of Change & Stability

"You're too stuck in your ways." "Our relationship has become stale." "Why don't you ever want to try anything new?" "Living with you is constant upheaval." "I never know who I'm going to meet on the other end of the phone." "When are you ever going to settle down?" Different versions of these questions arise in many marriages.

What do we do about those nagging questions? How do we decide how much change or how much stability is healthy? When you look more closely at developmental theory and at the physics of spiritual transformation, an interesting relationship between change and stability emerges. In order to develop, we have to learn to allow "change" and "stability" to be in a healthy, dynamic tension with one another, a tension that will ebb and flow, tighten on one end, and lighten up a little on the other. And we, as agents of conscious evolution, perfect the art of flexibility, seamlessly adjusting so we continually create the most supportive environment for higher development.

Evolutionary transformation is about emergence—the surfacing of new capacities that didn't exist before. It is also equally about integration—forming new personal and cultural habits around the higher qualities and capacities that have peeked through. The skills, conditions, pacing, and focus needed for both differ; yet both are essential for building a truly new and stable culture.

So what does that mean about our intimate relationships? What does that mean about navigating the rhythm and flow of our marriage? It means that when the need for consistency, commitment, and reliability asserts its head, we approach our needs and the needs of our spouses in a developmental context.

Facilitating emergence in ourselves and in others is one of the more highly developed human skills. It takes heart, patience, curiosity, and a light touch. Doing this together, with your partner, can fundamentally alter that contentious dynamic, "I want space to grow and change" and "But I want consistency and order" to a fruitful exploration of what it takes to foster the conditions of emergence. This brings a level of respect, appreciation, intimacy, and gratitude that is rare in our times—a beacon of what's possible between two people who love each other.

WHAT'S NEXT

Building Conscious Awareness

We explored the foundation of awareness, of unity consciousness, of the already fullness of Self. Lifting the veils of separation to peer into the brilliance of emptiness remains the foundation of spiritual awakening and this type of deep human development. As we've seen, from this immersion, we are able to better support and create together with our partners. At peace, we can let go, knowing we are, in essence, inherently complete. The skills and tools we have been working with illustrate practical ways we can extend our roots of Self, in that mysterious realization of

Oneness, fullness, that which is never separate from another.

As you work this in yourself, continue to reflect on how you can become increasingly familiar, intimate with that recognition that there is nothing missing. How can you become familiar with that posture in relationship to life where there is no fundamental need, hurt, or fear? Take time, make space for this. What practices are you curious to experiment with to support your love of this place of already fullness? The more we habituate ourselves to take root in this dimension of self, the more full we will experience ourselves to be. Manually reaffirming that dimension of Self, our intimacy will be permeated with a quality of freedom, space, innocence, and love.

How can you support your partner's experience of that dimension of self? What habits can you change in how you're relating to each other that will peel back the encroachment and create freedom and support for the recognition of Self? These are powerful contemplations to refer to over and over again. They challenge us to see how engaged a spiritual life we're living. How active are we with that dimension of the self? How much more engaged can we be? What are our habits of conversation, interaction, thought, and inquiry that support living an awakened life? Which inhibit and take away from that? As you put emphasis on this in your relationship, you're going to experience a change across the board. It's such a radical shift from a culture that promotes incessant need and lack.

We've also opened up an exploration of a different foundation for trust. What's a stronger and more reliable expression of trust in relationship? There are ways we look at others, waiting for them to prove themselves to us. This leads to separation, suspicion, and tension—the opposite of what we are hoping for. With an evolutionary and spiritual view on relationship and life, we lose the chip on our shoulders, becoming solid touchstones of trustworthiness to ourselves first.

Working together towards a greater aspiration creates a foundation for trust, mutuality, and an on-the-same-team spirit between us. How can you come together with your partner in a contemplation of mutual purpose? How can you refine your ability to articulate your life's mission, and adjust it so you have mid-term and long-term aspirations? How can you expect more and reach for a shared aim that's truly reflective of higher human capacities? How can you become intimate with a vast purpose that will provide a context and container for your life together with your partner?

Are you clear about your mission or vocation? Is your relationship to purpose something you truly identify with? As you struggle to articulate your highest goals you'll experience the crescendo swell of excitement, working together with your partner on something neither of you can see, smell, taste, or touch, and you have intimations that if you keep stretching, keep reaching, together you'll pull it from beyond the known into the present.

Shared purpose puts us on the same team with our partners, working together for the same goal. In any collective endeavor, when you're focused on the same end, you find creative and unusual ways of working together to achieve that goal. Rather than setting up a dynamic where we are at odds with our partners, where we want them to change or they want to change us, we're living with each other in a rhythm that is characterized by ease and immersion in current of evolution.

You can see how when you're directed by a goal that's way bigger than either of you, it makes space between you and your partner. It creates trust; we realize that to accomplish a goal as audacious as individual transformation, mystical realization, and evolutionary emergence, we're embracing a huge, subtle, and significant life mission. It opens room for challenges we might feel in ourselves or that our partners might be experiencing. We experience compassion, knowing the delicacy of human development. A living relationship will bubble with an undercurrent of joy. Over time, you'll experience movement, letting go, discovery, you'll actually see the development in yourself. What more supportive foundation can there be for our relationship to grow and for us to grow as individuals?

Let's briefly revisit the exploration of home. Are you ultimately resting in consciousness as home? Are we rich with our own experience of the spiritual heart, able to create an external expression of it, bring that into the world? Do we foster an environment where the qualities of spirit are what people experience when they are with us? Where our invitation of hospitality extends a message from the limitless generosity of the spiritual self?

As you reflect on how your images and ideals of home have changed over time, you'll start to see the influence of history on us. You'll start to see that some of the qualities that seem essential to have in your home are conditioned cultural programming that may have nothing to do with the spiritually awakened, future-seeking ideals you truly care about. We're all conditioned by layers and layers of culture. Conscious evolution means freely choosing what qualities we value and that support emergence. How are we conditioned to think about home? What would home be that really supports spiritual development?

And finally, our relationships flourish as we learn to negotiate the tides of change and stability, the extensions of ourselves, the periods of gestation and involution. This is one of the more challenging life skills to develop, one underestimated and underappreciated. As context and purpose take shape between us and our partners, and as we open in love, empathy, curiosity, and sensitivity, we'll begin to perfect the art of balance.

Closing Wishes

I encourage each and every one of you reading this book to value your intention to evolve your relationships into powerful pillars of a future-oriented, spiritual culture. These qualities support our collective development and our individual fulfillment. I hope that you continue to engage with these questions in a way that helps you experience a depth of trust, fulfillment, excitement, intimacy, love, complexity, and compassion in your relationship that leads to tremendous growth. And I look forward to meeting you someday and sharing these ideas and their fruits together. We can all be so much more than we are.

AMY EDELSTEIN

Amy Edelstein, author, educator, and public speaker is a powerful communicator of ideas and beliefs that help transform ourselves and the culture we live in. She teaches a spiritually awakened perspective and the significance of an evolutionary worldview. Engaging, sensitive, and insightful, Amy's mission is to support as many people as possible to grow beyond their own expectations.

Amy is the founder of the *Inner Strength Foundation*, which runs the *Mindfulness & Cultural Development Teen Program* serving over 800 high school students in Philadelphia Public Schools. She is also co-founder of Emergence Education, which produces educational materials for personal growth and the exploration of cultural development.

A Cornell University College Scholar, Amy has thirty years experience of spiritual practice, with a background in Judaism, Vedanta, and Buddhist spiritual philosophy, as well as in evolutionary spirituality, a contemporary philosophical perspective that connects individual transformation with a deep sense of responsibility for our collective future.

Amy was honored by the interfaith organization OUnI as the Wisdom chair for Evolutionary Spirituality in recognition of her 25 years of indepth exploration of collective emergence and postmodern cultural development with Andrew Cohen, as a senior editor for *What Is Enlightenment?* (later *EnlightenNext*) magazine. She is also the first interfaith minister of Evolutionary Spirituality.

In addition to this book, Amy is co-author of *Great Awakenings: Radical Visions of Spiritual Love & Evolution*, and is currently working on new book of poems *We All Come from Somewhere,* as well as a new release about evolutionary spirituality.

Learn more about Amy's work:

www.AmyEdelstein.com
info@amyedelstein.com

fb: facebook.com/AmyEdelstein.Educator

tw: @amyedelstein

www.ingramcontent.com/pod-product-compliance
Lightning Source LLC
Chambersburg PA
CBHW071506040426
42444CB00008B/1524